And What Do You Do?

And What Do You Do?

When Women Choose to Stay Home

LORETTA E. KAUFMAN AND MARY W. QUIGLEY

WILDCAT CANYON PRESS
A Division of Circulus Publishing Group, Inc.
Berkeley, California

Editorial Director: Roy M. Carlisle
Production Coordinator: Larissa Berry
Copyeditor: Jean Blomquist
Proofreader: Shirley Coe
Cover Design: Eleanor Reagh
Author photo by Joe Henson
Interior Design and Typesetting: Margaret Copeland—Terragraphics
Typographic Specifications: Body text set in 11.75 Bembo. Heads set in Mrs. Eaves Roman.

Printed in Canada

Cataloging-in-Publication Data
Kaufman, Loretta, 1944-
    And what do you do? : when women choose to stay home/Loretta
Kaufman and Mary Quigley.
        p. cm.
    Includes bibliographical references.
    ISBN 1-885171-40-4 (alk. paper)
    1. Housewives—United States 2. Wives—Effect of husbands
employment on—United States. 3. Sex role—United States. 4. Work
and family—United States. I. Quigley, Mary, 1949- II. Title

HQ759 .K3477 2000
305.43'649—dc21
                                                            00-021158

Distributed to the trade by Publishers Group West
10 9 8 7 6 5 4 3 2 1

Contents

Dedication

to Vic and Frank
for sharing our vision and
helping us achieve our dream

Acknowledgments

We are deeply grateful to the many wives and mothers across the country who shared their heartfelt thoughts and feelings with us whether face-to-face, on the phone, or through countless e-mail missives. Without their help, this book would not have been possible.

Like many books, this one evolved slowly at first and then kicked into high gear. Various people, from friends to colleagues, helped along the way.

In the beginning stages, Robert Gottlieb and his associates at the William Morris Agency gave invaluable guidance for first-time authors.

For believing in us and our idea, we thank the triumvirate at Wildcat Canyon Press: Tamara Traeder for her early enthusiastic support, Roy M. Carlisle for encouraging us from the proposal stage onward and for his editorial insights, and Julie Bennett for helping us refine and focus our idea as well as for her marketing abilities. Thanks go also to the rest of the Wildcat Canyon gang, especially Nenelle Bunnin and Leyza Yardley, for helping sustain our bicoastal relationship.

Many others helped along the way with solid suggestions. Michael Norman, Ann Matthews, Nancy Hass, and John Wright contributed editorial expertise in the early stages of this book. Judith Serrin also did an outstanding job of editing on a tight deadline.

We welcomed advice from many others—some friends,

some colleagues, some both—including Adam Berkowitz, Terri Brooks, Marian Gormley, Susie Israelson, Susannah Kellems, Lynn Langway, Rebecca Raphael, Debbie Schneider, Eli Segal, Phyllis Segal, Bill Serrin, Elizabeth Shreve, Mitch Stephens, and Patty Weiner.

Dr. Xavier Amador and Dr. Willa Bernhard supplied background and context while we were doing our initial research. Profs. Kathleen Gerson of New York University, W. Jay Hughes of Georgia Southern University, Myra Strober of Stanford University, and Linda Stroh of Loyola University, provided additional perspective on marital and workplace issues.

Our agent, Alice Martell, spurred us from the proposal stage onward with sage advice. Publicists Lynn Goldberg and Megan Underwood of Goldberg McDuffie Communications ably helped us launch the book.

We are very appreciative to our talented assistant, Carrie Havranek, for the twenty-something sensibility she brought to our seemingly endless drafts, to say nothing of her research and transcribing skills. Her sense of humor always cheered us when we needed it most.

Our support system of friends, who listened to us talk on and on about this project, deserve a special thank-you. Loretta thanks Annie Gilbar for having faith in her as a fledgling journalist. She also thanks her friends and "family" in New York and L.A. for their enthusiasm. For both their friendship and sharing their feelings as wives and mothers, Mary thanks Silvia Rowney and Vivien Orbach Smith, who also gave invaluable editorial input from the earliest stages to the completion of the book.

Of course, without the patience and support of our families, this book would not have been possible.

Loretta: I am grateful to my husband, Vic, for his endless love. He has encouraged everything I have done, most of all getting this book off the ground. His enthusiasm and wisdom have always been my source of inspiration. And thanks to Liz and Jimmy, my terrific thirty-something children who, besides showing great excitement for their mom's project, gave us insight into the choices their friends face about family and work.

Mary: I am grateful to my parents, John and Dorothy Whalen, for demonstrating the importance of family and hard work. My three wonderful children, Brendan, Sean and Colleen, were the inspiration for this book in many ways. Even though "the book" seemed at times like an additional—and not always welcome—person in our family, they were incredibly understanding. My husband, Frank, read every draft, providing exhaustive and insightful commentary. I will be forever grateful for his constant encouragement and his love.

Preface

We met as student and teacher: Loretta, back to school after a hiatus of several years, was a student in Mary's graduate journalism course at NYU. A friendship blossomed, followed by several joint writing projects. One day, over cappuccino in a Greenwich Village café, we ruminated about writing books on marriage and motherhood and work. To our surprise, our thoughts were running on parallel paths. So we concluded, why not "job share" a book and bounce ideas off each other rather than working solo? We saw where our two proposals intersected, and we came up with the notion of exploring the difficult choice that women make when they put their careers on hold for the sake of their husbands and families. How do women come to terms with their often conflicted feelings about this new way of life? One way to approach this might have been through a sociological study. But we're not sociologists; we are journalists. So we went into the field, storming the front lines to find out who was home. When we rang the doorbells, so to speak, we found that not many women were home. Instead they were busy with family and friends, volunteer and paid part-time work.

We wanted to go beyond six degrees of separation so we e-mailed dozens of women across the country who are linked by a wide variety of at-home organizations. As one woman led to another, we tapped a well of thoughts and feelings that had been ignored—we dare say, even maligned—by our culture at large. The amazing women we found at home broke every stereotype, and they were anxious to tell their stories. At one point we had a waiting list of wives who wanted to be interviewed. Through a combination of in-person, telephone, and e-mail interviews, we developed our own network and started a discussion that revealed layers and layers of previously unspoken attitudes and beliefs.

Their stories were our own: Loretta says, "When I married my high school sweetheart, I had never met a movie star nor did I think I would. I could no sooner picture myself hobnobbing with the Hollywood A-list than meeting the Queen of England. Yet by 1987—when my husband, Vic, became CEO of Columbia Pictures Entertainment, the parent company of Columbia Pictures and TriStar Pictures—I had done both.

"Even though Hollywood meant dinners with Barbara Streisand and Demi and Bruce, we opted to make our home on Long Island, believing it was the better place to raise our two children. Carpools, finances, in-laws, school, kids: they were all part of the recipe for my daily living. So while Vic was jetting coast to coast, I manned mission control at home. Together—and that's the operative word here—we decided that there couldn't be two fast-trackers in our family. I would put my career plans on hold and my dream of a graduate degree on the back burner, making Vic and the children a priority . . . for a while. It was an easy call for me. This was his time; my time would come. How could I be so sure? From the day we married in 1965, I always knew that our marriage was a partnership, based on mutual respect, love, and trust. In a marriage, like any partnership, things are not always evenly split down the middle and not always balanced. During those Columbia years—his years—I knew in my heart that Vic appreciated everything I did to make his frenetic existence easier, and I have to admit that I still like hearing him say, 'I couldn't do it without you.'"

Mary recalls, "When Loretta casually mentioned her idea for the book, I knew exactly what she meant. I too had made many personal and career decisions based on making my family the priority.

"I was raised in a family with four daughters who were all encouraged to work and have careers. The women's movement echoed my parents, who told me I could do anything. So work I did, in publishing and public relations, before going back to school in 1978 to get my master's degree in journalism. Two years later, just after my thirtieth birthday and nine years of marriage, my first child was born. My husband and I had approached marriage as a partnership right from the beginning. I supported him through law school, and he helped me get through graduate school while I was working full-time. Together we decided that vacations and eating dinners out were not a priority. In fact they weren't even an option. We jointly decided that I would stay home to care for our son and the other children we planned. Yes, economics played a role; Frank made more money than I did. More important, I wanted to stay home. First, after reading all those parenting books, I was convinced it was crucial for the children. Second, I thought I'd enjoy being a full-time mother. And third, while I liked my job, I was ready to try a new direction and it seemed like a perfect time to stop and reassess my career.

"Like most new mothers, I was overwhelmed by the many responsibilities and could do little more than care for the baby for the first six months. But gradually, as my son settled into a predictable schedule, I suddenly had more free time than I ever imagined. It occurred to me that 'staying home' didn't mean I had to stay in the house every minute, so when the NYU journalism chairman asked me to teach one course, it seemed like a perfect fit. About the same time, *Newsday* was starting a new city edition and needed part-time reporters. I began covering stories once or twice a week in the evenings while my husband cared for our son. Teaching one course at NYU and freelance writing continued for ten years, through another son and a daughter. As my children grew, I took a job at NYU with more responsibility—and flexible hours—that allowed my back-burnered career to slowly heat up to a level comfortable for me and my family."

As we conducted our interviews, we found that many wives were still struggling with the same decisions that we had agonized over. Woman after woman actually thanked us for writing this book, for giving them a chance to reveal their feelings, and for giving validation to—and celebrating—their choices. The result is, we hope, a volume that speaks not only for us, but also for every other woman who has paused for a moment before answering, "And what do you do?"

1

Rewriting
the Rules

I T'S LIKE A DIRTY LITTLE SECRET that people whisper but
refuse to publicly acknowledge. Married life starts off equal:
his career, her career. But as jobs jump to the fast track, as
babies come along, as life begins to move at a blinding pace,
sooner or later a couple realizes that something has to give, and
often it's the wife's career. So what's a woman to do? In conversations with wives from coast to coast, we found a surprising number of savvy, educated, take-charge women who have
courageously carved out a unique role that is part traditional,
part feminist. Without any fanfare or media attention, women
across America have rewritten the rules and found creative,
rewarding ways to combine marriage and mothering, work
and play. Yes, they have it all . . . but not all at the same time.

Little recognition has been given to the 7.7 million married mothers with children under age eighteen who don't work . . . by choice! Another 5 million married mothers work part-time in an effort to integrate—not juggle—some work with their primary concern, family life.[1]

In one sense, these women are traditional wives and mothers, choosing to make their husbands and children a priority, either by staying home full-time or cutting back to part-time work. In another sense, they are very nontraditional. Steeped in feminism, they certainly are not second-class citizens in their marriages or families. They didn't trade their brains for baby bottles. But when marriage and motherhood caused their priorities to shift, they were bold and brave enough to make radical changes in their lives. Yes, many made those changes with a great deal of angst and conflict. As they improvised their new roles the doubts disappeared, and now many bring an energy and enthusiasm to their at-home lives that spill out into the wider community.

We hear a great deal about the struggles of working mothers. Institutes and studies examine their problems. Magazines talk about "juggling" a job and kids. In movies and on television, the perfect mom is a fashionably dressed executive. What we don't see portrayed very often is the mom who turns in her briefcase for her family. We don't hear much about the 56 percent of women with children age seventeen or younger who rank being a good wife and mother as the primary measure of their success in life—ahead of wealth, power, fame, influence, or knowledge.[2] While the so-called "mommy wars" rage, millions of women are quietly withdrawing from the front lines, often feeling like part of an underground organization, linked by local at-home groups and e-mail. At the turn of the twenty-first century, the part-feminist, part-traditional woman is stunned that staying at home is counterculture.

Let's be honest, a career change to be supportive of husband and family is politically incorrect—a reason why this "trendlet," as demographers might call it, is not getting much media attention. These women chose a path that, as more than one woman noted, made them feel like social outcasts. A response of "I take care of my husband and children" is not likely to impress people who ask the standard conversation opener, "And what do you do?"

Who is the woman at home? Surprisingly, the stereotype is still some souped-up version of June Cleaver. That simply is not the case. These same women grew up with feminism as their mantra; most planned on combining work and family. And therein lies the key issue: no alternative was ever considered. Popular culture, many believe, summarily dismisses at-home life as a waste of a well-educated mind.

We have found an amazing group of women whose stories read like fiction, ranging from the Navy pilot's twenty-six-year-old wife who sent her husband off to the Persian Gulf, to an ex–Broadway dancer and wife of a soap opera star, to a surgeon's wife who provides a home-away-from-home for his transplant patients and their families. These women differ in many ways, from demographics to political attitudes. Gradations on a scale, some are more traditional than others. Some plan to return to work five or ten years down the road. Others believe, as the bumper sticker proclaims, "Dorothy was right. There's no place like home," and there they plan to stay. Yet, despite the differences, we found that remarkably similar attitudes, opinions, and beliefs cropped up repeatedly in our conversations. What emerged, as the women described the thinking behind their decisions, was a shared subconscious of sorts, with its own new vocabulary: partnering, back-burnering, retooling, taking turns, gift giving.

A variety of personal circumstances propelled the move to the home front: the first baby, a husband's all-consuming career, exhaustion from working and then doing the "second shift," a career that was not as fulfilling as expected. For some, it was the sudden dawning that while a career can be put on hold, childhood can't; it's a one-time offer that expires very quickly. The change came for others when they decided that passing their husbands like ships in the night was not the relationship they had envisioned. After attempting to combine work and family, still others concluded that life should be more than a 9-to-5 job and 5-to-9 child care. Many gradually came to the understanding that an education is not only training for a job; it's training for life. So one by one, after building careers, some for a decade or more, these young women put their doubts and fears aside and went home. They were surprised to learn that the adage is true: When the wind slams shut one door, it blows open yet another.

Ranging in age from their mid-twenties to late forties, these wives see themselves as partners—not servants or secretaries—with their husbands in an adventure called family life. In the 1990s and beyond, family life resembles a complex corporate enterprise. These wonder women rightfully claim that they "do it all," including finances (from checkbooks to investing), operations (from housing to lifestyle), and strategic planning (from number of children to instilling core values). Because of their previous professional experience, many function as in-residence consultants for their husbands on everything from hiring decisions to office politics. From the outside looking in, the role might not appear equal, but inside the marriage there is a basic understanding that each partner is indispensable to the other. Money is not the way to keep score. The wife's contribution is not taken for granted: it is acknowledged, applauded, and valued by her husband.

In writing this book, we often felt like Lewis and Clark, the explorers who invented terms for flora and fauna they discovered in the uncharted West. Our language does not have a word, name, or label that describes these women or honors their choice. Housewives? We won't even touch that. The very fact that there is no term is a good indication that they are being ignored. So we asked these women to characterize themselves. Many responded, reflecting their previous corporate lives, "I am the family CEO." Others used terms such as "new-fashioned wife" or "new traditional wife." We chose to use "family CEO" and "new traditional wife" as they encompass most aspects of this multidimensional role.

Where did this new generation of women come from? Some evolved, others made a conscious decision to stay at home, and still others kicked and screamed before realizing they had to make a change for their sanity as well as that of their families. Many found the transition difficult because at-home wives are not only ignored, they are often dismissed as not deserving attention . . . or worse. "Culturally, the skewed attitudes about at-home motherhood seem to proliferate," writes Cecelie Berry in *Salon*'s "Mothers Who Think" online column. "*The New York Times* and *The Wall Street Journal* have published articles referring to at-home mothers as executive 'status symbols,' a label that demeans the work we do and the sacrifices we make. In movies like *One True Thing* and *Stepmom*, the mother who raises her children at home fades away, swanlike, stricken by cancer, while the younger career woman flourishes. These movies function like health warnings: Work makes women stronger; stay-at-home motherhood is carcinogenic."[3]

Many slowly came to a new way of viewing life, like Betty Walter, a thirty-seven-year-old mother of two and former Environmental Protection Agency program analyst. "I think that as a young woman going to college, graduate school, and entrenched on the career path, I was inside the box that the feminist movement had created for me," she says. "I couldn't think beyond it. I valued myself in terms of the work that I did. But motherhood has showed me that the box is too confining, and that there is more to life than a good title, a great career, and money. The same is true with regard to being a wife. Being married is a continual challenge. To succeed, you have to plow through, bite your tongue, swallow your pride, and look to the greater good of the family unit. These are not bad things, because they ultimately reveal what matters most in life—each other."

Critics often counter that staying home is a choice only for six-figure income couples. The numbers prove otherwise. In families with both mother and father employed full-time and year-round the median income is $51,950. The median for married-couple families with children below age eighteen and a nonemployed mother is $36,786.[4] (Keep in mind these figures do not include the incomes of the 5.5 million wives who work part-time, ranging from one to thirty-four hours a week.) Obviously for some, this decision to stay at home borders on economic hardship. For others it means living on a tight budget and forgoing "necessities," such as cable TV or resort vacations. For still others, the economic impact is nil and the question centers solely on whether the wife is willing to put aside her career. Whatever the tax bracket, the choice to take a "timeout" is made by both husband and wife—as partners. Most marriages start as dual-income ventures: two incomes, two people. Suddenly, often after the birth of the first or second baby, the arrangement becomes one-income, three or four people—a deal many men didn't sign on for. Frankly, some husbands are not willing to take on that extra financial burden. Just as it takes a special type of woman to become a new traditional wife, this arrangement takes an uncommon man, one who believes so strongly in their partnership that he is willing to assume the full fiscal responsibility.

Staying at home, taking time out, is not for all wives. Financially, it is out of the question for some women. Others find more satisfaction in the office than at home. For many women, the changing nature of work over the past decade drives the decision. Americans today work longer hours than any industrialized country.[5] In many ways corporations now demand more than ever: sixty-hour weeks are the norm; frequent travel is expected at all levels of management; thanks to e-mail, beepers, and cell phones the employee is never off duty. Many women told us of frantic phone calls: six o'clock had come and gone and the children were still at day care.

Whose turn—husband's or wife's—was it to leave the office? Too often that scenario was the rule rather than the exception. This is not a way to live. Of course, some critics may ask why the husband doesn't quit his job and become Mr. Mom. The answer is simple: all the women we spoke to agreed that they *wanted* to stay home, and some admitted that their husbands were not-so-secretly envious.

The cadres of women who are willing to make this courageous choice to stay home are imbued with a strong sense of self. And it does take courage to assume a role that some sociologists call "economic suicide." While this kind of marital partnership often leads to stronger, happier marriages, there are certainly no guarantees. And, community property laws aside, a woman could end up in a financially precarious situation if her husband leaves her. The new traditional wife is willing to assume that risk, bolstered by belief in her own abilities. Princeton grad Alison Carlson, a forty-four-year-old mother of three boys who recently moved to Reston, Virginia, echoes the sentiments of many wives: "I lived on my own and supported myself for nine years, including three years of law school, before getting married so I am confident that I can be financially independent whenever necessary. I don't have to go out and prove it every day—I've been there and done that and know I can do it again!"

No, it is not an easy decision. But, ultimately, the rewards are many. Through our interviews, we show how and why these choices enhance lives: how "partnering" gives wives an equal voice in marriage; why they "back-burner" their careers, some for a few years, others for a decade or more; how they "retool" those job skills into new, emotionally rewarding work, both paid and volunteer; how they negotiate with their husbands to "take turns" in terms of career priorities; how their "gift" of love and time to their families comes back to them tenfold.

◦° A New Vision of Partnership ℅

What sets these women apart from wives of previous generations is that they strongly believe they are *partners* with their husbands in marriage. Each spouse plays a role in making family life work. Many women we talked with emphasized that they set the tone and pace of family life just as a CEO does for a business. Well-educated and wise to the ways of the work world, the wives make more than mundane household decisions. Many often control the family finances right down to investing, refinancing mortgages, buying—and selling—houses, overseeing major renovations, all with little consultation from their husbands. Indeed, they have caused a change in the mind-set of many home contractors. "Nowadays when a woman says, 'I'll discuss it with my husband,' it usually means she is stalling me," says one building contractor. "These ladies are the ones who make the decisions, not the men."

The wives' efforts are valued and applauded by husbands. No, not all the time, but often enough so the wife feels that she is a full partner with her husband in the life they have created for themselves and their children. The wife of a surgeon told how her husband profusely thanked her and called her to the podium to share an award honoring his work. "He publicly thanked me, saying I deserved the award as much as he did," says Erica Miller.

❧ Letting It Simmer ❧

It's a simple analogy. When we put a pot on the *back burner*, we don't turn off the heat; *we turn it down and let it simmer.* That's exactly what psychologist Deborah Williams did when she put her hard-won practice aside for her husband, Herb, during his peak playing years in the NBA. Schoolteacher Joan Waldman took a sixteen-year break to raise two sons and provide support for her husband, and she returned with an energy and creativity that helped her land a position as principal.

What women want is work that works, work that fits into their new lifestyle. They don't want the work to dominate their personal lives, and they are driven to find a better way. Some—especially doctors, lawyers, and other professionals—stay in the same field and cut back on their hours, still keeping their hand in. Other women leave work completely until the time is right to return. The new traditional wife doesn't turn her back on her career. Instead, she finds ways to keep it simmering.

❧ Creativity with a Twist ❧

Because the new traditional wives have considerable work—and world—experience, they don't "hang it up" when they're no longer on the 7:03 train to the city. Instead they *retool* and use their talents in creative new ways.

After more than a decade of writing catchy commercials at an advertising agency, Nina Salkin, a rabbi's wife, now uses those same skills in other ways—from editing a newsletter for rabbinical wives to producing a curriculum on Israel for her son's elementary school.

Across the country the story is the same: numerous preschools now have pension plans for their teachers, thanks to "volunteer" CPA moms; church and community groups benefit from long-range planning and new fund-raising strategies devised by women who used to do the same for corporations. One mother we know capitalized on her organizational skills to coordinate volunteers for months of daily dinners for a family with a terminally ill mother. These women are not "wasting" their education as some critics might claim. They are using their training for other than paid work.

⤳ Shifting Gears for the Turns ⤳

Most new traditional wives make the decision to change their lives having an understanding with their husbands about taking turns. At some point, their own careers will get priority. It may not be the same career they left. Many women see this hiatus as a time to explore new avenues for other types of work. For some it is work that is emotionally as well as economically rewarding. For others it is simply work that fits into their lives.

Preschool teacher Margo Litzenberg found it impossible as a young mother to continue working while her husband was flying Navy planes in the Persian Gulf for six months at a time. That doesn't mean she never plans to return to teaching. She expects that one day her husband will support her goal to get a Ph.D. just as she supported his dreams.

Admittedly it's not an easy transition back to school or to the office, even one in a side room of the house. But these wives are counting on their husbands to help them ease the transition and help them find a new way of work.

⌒ Learning the Arts of Gratitude ⌒ and Sacrifice

Sociologist Arlie Hochschild writes, "When couples struggle, it is seldom over simply who does what. Far more often, it is over the *giving and receiving of gratitude.*"[6] We found that many women, as academics have documented, are by their very nature nurturers, taking great satisfaction in caring for others. Those we talked to emphasized that they relished giving a gift of their talents and time to their husbands and children.

The wife of a doctor who works fourteen-hour days, Erica Miller, says, "His work is so important that we agreed this is the way our life is going to be. It's our arrangement. I like to be nurturing. I like being a wife and a mother and making a home, so I do see that an important part of our relationship is for me to be there for him, and I have made that commitment to him."

Some critics might say she is making an incredible "sacrifice." If the supposed sacrifice is approached as partnering, it is no sacrifice at all. Moving from the Midwest to Arizona, Sharon Beeler put her own career on hold to help her husband establish his business as a Western artist. "We were busy [working] toward the same goal, so I didn't feel that I was sacrificing anything," she says. "Joe's career is what we're into and it takes both of us."

⤲ Forty Years of Mixed Signals ⤳

In 1963, Betty Friedan's *The Feminine Mystique* gave women permission to throw off their aprons. Seven years of cultural change later, *Life* magazine proclaimed the emergence of the women's movement with a cover photo of masses of women marching for equal rights in the nation's capital. One generation after another, women flocked to college and professional school and then joined the work force believing that they had to imitate their male counterparts step for step. Almost twenty years passed before another magazine, *Time*, acknowledged that the feminist movement had sputtered with a cover story that proclaimed, "In the '80s they tried to have it all. Now they have just plain had it." It's as if women were driving down a highway one way, were told to reverse course, and then miles later were told, "No, that's the wrong way too."

The 1990s left women to figure it out for themselves, with no apparent "right" way. If a woman goes to medical school and chooses after a time to cut back her hours to stay at home, she's blasted by some feminists as a defector from the movement that fought for her to get a spot in medical school in the first place. If a woman stays home to care for her family, she's often faced with the taunts: "What do you do all day?" or "Isn't your mind going to mush?" Yet ask women who work full-time jobs and care for husbands and family, and most will agree that it's almost an impossible task. As Arlie Hochschild notes in her book *The Second Shift*, the extra burden that working women carry is often "the job that tears the family apart," amounting to the annual equivalent of an extra month of twenty-four hour days of work.[7]

13

The decade saw a continuation of the much publicized mommy wars. That battlefield was lined on one side by neo-feminists, who want all women to have babies first and then a career, if at all. They waged a war with books and TV talk shows against the hard-line feminists who believe that any woman not working full-time is a traitor to the cause of gender equality. Some feminists argue that those moms-at-home are part of the reason that women are still making only seventy-five cents for every dollar earned by men. Yet some women—the new traditional wives—managed to find what could be called a third way. This solution was first proposed in 1986 in *Sequencing,* a book by Arlene Rossen Cardozo, who suggested women divide their lives into three stages: full-time work, full-time mothering, integration of both.[8] The concept of sequencing never received the widespread media attention it deserved. Perhaps it was an idea before its time. Instead, most of the women we talked to charged full steam into their careers with blinders on. Only when they hit a mental wall that signaled a need for change did they look to a serendipitous solution rather a long-range plan.

Who Wrote This Script?

How then do some women manage to successfully navigate change? That's one of the questions we sought to explore in this book. The short answer for most of the women we interviewed is that marriage is a joint commitment by both spouses to a certain way of life and that, for a period of time, a husband's career and child-rearing take priority. Sometimes that situation lasts for only five or ten years. In other marriages it has evolved an ongoing lifestyle.

When we marry, many of us do not have uppermost in our minds the notion of making the marriage, rather than the individuals, paramount. That idea evolves over time. Sometimes the seeds are planted in childhood. Erica Miller idealized a loving and nurturing family life with lots of traditional festivities. On the other hand, Maureen Canary saw the lights of Broadway as her goal, not a house in Connecticut with a dog and two children and an actor husband.

Where do our expectations for marriage come from and how does that influence the choices we make? In part, our expectations rise out of what Dr. Xavier Amador,[9] a New York psychologist who counsels men and women about relationships, calls our "marriage script." Translated, a marriage script is the vision in our mind's eye of what our marriage will be like: a white house with a picket fence and lots of happy kids, or arguing, bitter parents, or mothers juggling job and family, exhausted all the time. Dr. Amador, author of *Being Single in a Couples' World*, points out that the problem with the marriage script is that it is often out of date, "written" in our childhood years, and not based on present-day reality. For women in particular, the marriage script is troublesome because the basic assumptions regarding work, independence, and responsibilities keep shifting as our culture's view of the politically correct role of women evolves. So a woman in her mid-thirties who started thinking about marriage and family and career in the early 1980s may have the do-it-all model engrained in her mind. Yet reality brings a different set of circumstances that makes do-it-all impossible.

Dr. Amador notes, "Women are getting two different cultural scripts about who they should be in America. A lot of baby boomers grew up getting one script and then what emerged was this other script. And your personal script has everything to do with what happened in your own family. So if you feel that your mother gave up way too much and she resented it, [you think that] if you do the same, you [will] lose your identity. A lot of women I've worked with are really worried about losing their identity, that they'll get married and they'll become Mrs. So-and-So, that they're not going to be themselves. And some [other] women are not afraid of that."

This book validates the feelings and choices of millions of women, who have often been given the cold shoulder before, but now, at the dawn of the new millennium, reflect a shift in the culture. We found women who were deeply in love with their husbands; women who had made their marriage and children a priority, a silent minority who chose to "go against the grain." For some of these women, it means supporting their husbands' career choices while placing their own on hold. For others, it means more than being supportive, it is coping with difficult and sometimes disturbing situations. It is an ordeal to uproot a family when your husband is transferred, to go to parts unknown. But dozens of women told us that the unexpected rewards they got back were far greater than the ones they gave. Some of the rewards were tangible: unexpected business opportunities, comfortable homes. Others were not quantitative: increased self-esteem, a better understanding of who they are as women, and a greater connection with their spiritual side.

A hallmark of this group of women is that after ten, fifteen, even twenty-five years of marriage, they still admire and respect their husbands. We found women who make a commitment to putting the marriage before individual needs, who approach marriage as larger than the sum of the parts, and they are eager to talk about it. They have, dare we say, good news to tell and we share it with you now . . .

2

Going against the Grain

Mention Ozzie and Harriet to a woman born after 1965 and she might give you a puzzled look. The much maligned stay-at-home mom and her picture-perfect family are not cultural icons to these young women. The baby busters and Gen X grew up with the *Happy Days* Cunninghams on one end of the familial spectrum and Murphy Brown, an in-your-face, artificially inseminated single mom at the other. Is it any wonder young women today are often confused and conflicted about their roles?

After women finally made their way onto the pages of history and literature textbooks, little girls began to talk about growing up to be astronauts and presidents and lawyers and business executives. This was the first generation to be told

"Why be a nurse when you can be a doctor?" They flocked to college, and not to get the infamous "MRS." degree of their mothers' generation. In 1960, male college students outnumbered females more than two to one. By 1996, women made up almost 60 percent of college students.[1]

This generation of do-it-all, have-it-all young women applauded the advances gained in the hard-fought feminist battles of the '60s and early '70s. Many of them grabbed the opportunities offered and went on to climb the ladder to success. "From the time I was in high school, I was very career oriented. My goal was to work, make money, and be self-sufficient," says Shelley Draheim, thirty-six, of Burke, Virginia, who worked as a government relations specialist and researcher. She echoes a sentiment shared by millions of young women who jump on a career treadmill and rarely slow down, not even breaking stride for marriage and then baby, who is wheeled right to the day-care center. Endurance, patience, flexibility, and a Palm Pilot are needed to maintain that schedule. And even that's not enough. Often after a few months of trying to "do it all," many mothers are left feeling that they are holding down two jobs—one at the office and the other at home—and doing neither very well.

A 1997 study, "Motherhood Today: A Tougher Job Less Ably Done" by The Pew Center for The People and The Press, found the biggest challenge mothers face is dealing with time pressures attendant to being a mother as well as a worker and a wife. The study also found that American women overwhelmingly believe that the job of raising children these days is harder than it was a generation ago.[2] The added stress of work is not the only reason. "What's changed is our education and our society's view of what constitutes a good parent," says Candace Hill, forty-two, of Evanston, Illinois, who had worked for almost twenty years before having children. "Women of my age were in the workplace, had performance evaluations, were measured by a job well done. We now expect that of ourselves in our parenting. It's professionalized parenthood. That's reflected in the view by society that if something happens to our children it is our fault because we were not as protective as we should have been."

Even with the increased difficulties and expectations of parenthood, many women must work full-time to help support their families financially. For other women in the middle-income-and-above bracket, the decision to continue full-time work is based on wanting a certain lifestyle rather than an economic necessity. The often-cited statistic is that half of American mothers with children under eighteen work full-time outside the home.[3] That also means half do not.

The women who don't work are often ignored by the media. While they may not get much attention, they have struggled just as hard as working women to fashion a lifestyle that suits them and their families. In certain social circles where the family can withstand the loss of the wife's income, it has become socially acceptable—though not politically correct; that's pushing the envelope too far—to say, "I'm taking a few years off to raise the kids." Still, these women don't advertise their temporary exit from the paid work world because it is not something that gets applauded, especially in big cities like New York, L.A., or Washington, DC. Reporter Tracy Thompson wrote in *The Washington Post* about her maternity leave, "Showing up at a social gathering as just a mom is like showing up in your underwear: revealing and chilling."[4]

Politically Incorrect and Proud of It

It takes courage to go against the grain of what society expects of an educated woman. What we mean by going against the grain is being unconventional. The conventional expectation for a wife and mother today is that she works outside the home. To do otherwise is countercultural. When Alison Carlson, the Princeton grad, back-burnered her prestigious law career, the financial fallout was nothing compared to the social pressure that she felt: "I have often been a maverick in things I have done in my life. But I am surprised that in the 1990s staying at home makes me a maverick. I'm so sick of hearing intelligent, committed moms at home derided by modern feminists and the media. By suggesting that people in my position have made choices because we're unconsciously influenced by some patriarchal system, or really oppressed and don't know it, the media and feminists are undercutting their own argument. If that argument is true, then some of the best and brightest are stupid and duped. These stay-home moms want a certain kind of family life. They want to instill values, and if that means a more moderate income, they are willing to make tremendous sacrifices to do it."

Sometimes even friends and families are not supportive. "My mother and father were completely opposed and were aghast that I was giving up my career . . . everything I had worked for," says Jayme Holaway Hicks, thirty-six, of Ponte Vedra Beach, Florida. "I found myself in those first few months very defensive about my decision. People would ask me what I did for a living and I would respond with 'I used to be a stockbroker.' Now I proudly state that I am a 'Mama . . . and CEO of my household.'"

Opting to "stand by your man" is politically incorrect . . . except in a Tammy Wynette tune. The idea that a wife makes personal decisions based on what is best for her husband seems like fingernails scratching a blackboard. Some women would never dare to advertise they back-burnered their careers for the sake of their husbands and families. Why? Because there's still an attitude adrift in our culture that if a woman doesn't work full-time and cuts back for her family, it automatically means she is going to revert to some 1950s Donna Reed prototype, cleaning the house in high heels. The media does not glorify—or even recognize—the supportive wife. *Home Improvement*, the last TV sitcom to humorously portray the mother-father-2.5 kids American family, slipped into the network history books in the spring of 1999. "This show was created to celebrate the American family, and I'm not sure you can do that in the same way now," executive producer Matt Williams told *The New York Times.*[5]

That media attitude annoys Jennifer Ransdell, thirty-four, of Chicago. "I do get tired of being bombarded with TV and movies promoting 'working' mothers and treating most at-home moms like they are somehow behind the times," she says. "I try to prevent feeling negative pressure by surrounding myself with those who think as I do—that your children and husband have to come first."

Certainly Jennifer's notion infiltrates the public mind-set. Scouting around for at-home moms to interview for this book, we encountered more than one acquaintance who sniffed, "I don't have any friends like that." A women's group refused to let us join their meeting because they didn't want to advertise their personal situations. We discovered a stay-at-home-wife stereotype: "Don't they play a lot of tennis and shop constantly?" a colleague asked.

The new traditional wife challenges that stereotype by going against the grain politically and socially. When Alison attended her twentieth year reunion at Princeton, she marched in an alumni parade with a placard that read: "I practice alternative dispute resolution . . . at home with my three sons." Alison recalls the varied reactions: "Several classmates came up to me—and there were lots of extremely successful people in my class—and said they felt out of place because they're moms-at-home and felt inferior. With older alumni there were pockets of applause, and with the younger section of students the sign would catch their eye. You could see their thought process saying, 'Now that's a different idea.'"

☙ Surviving Career Suicide ❧

The new traditional wife goes against the grain in many other ways too. She is told that it's economic suicide to quit her job. Yet many explore new interests at home and discover rewarding work, paid and unpaid. Women are told that there's a prescribed career path to follow and that any deviation is perilous. Yet we met woman after woman who, despite following unconventional paths, successfully returned to the work world. Let's give these courageous women credit. They were steeped in role models and feminist ideas since preschool. They don't lose that just because they're not pounding a computer sixty hours a week for a corporation anymore. Oldsmobile once marketed cars to a younger audience with the slogan: "This is not your father's Oldsmobile." The same is true here: This is not you mother's mind-set. These are women who are in control of their own destinies; they make their own choices, even when those choices are criticized.

We both have endured disapproval of our career strategies. After five years of teaching part-time at New York University, Mary decided not to apply for a tenure track opening and to continue as an adjunct. One colleague after another questioned the sanity of her decision. Mary rattles off a list of practical reasons for turning down the offer, from having a husband who worked long hours to living twenty-plus miles from NYU. There was also a philosophical reason: "More is not always better," she says. "At that point in my life, I was not willing to give priority to my job. I was in my thirties. I had two small boys and was considering a third child. I had a sixty-year-old house that I wanted to renovate. I wanted to continue writing for a local newspaper. And I had just seen a colleague put in several years of sixty-hour weeks to get tenure at the expense of her personal life. The bottom line was that I knew I could still be satisfied with my career even if I wasn't going to be chair of my department anytime soon."

Mary made the decision to be a new traditional wife more than twenty years ago. She chose to have a career, but one in which she was at the controls. When her sons were in school all day, she took a part-administrative, part-teaching position in the journalism department that allowed her a flexible schedule. Even so, there were concessions because she worked. "I gave up a social life," Mary says. "I turned down invitations. A group of neighborhood women had a birthday club and went out to dinner regularly to celebrate. I often couldn't do that because I felt on the days I was working, I shouldn't go out at night. Other friends asked me to join a tennis group and I declined. For me, it was my husband and children first and then my job. There were no regrets. It was my choice."

For Mary, tailoring a career that jibes with her family life works best. Other women we spoke to decided to back-burner their careers, putting them on hold for a number of years. Admittedly, for a young wife the decision to back-burner a career can be an agonizing choice that comes only after months of internal conflict, months of arguments playing back and forth in her head. It's a tough call and one that can cause resentment. For these women, a career is not a choice. It is a given. In keeping with their view of marriage as a partnership, both husband and wife contemplate the decision to put the wife's career on hold and to stay home. They envision a certain quality of life for themselves and their children. What changes do they need to make to achieve it? They conclude (Mr. Mom notwithstanding) that the wife, for a variety of reasons, is better suited to cutting back or even foregoing her work life for a period of time. What often is not publicly acknowledged is that the decision is also made in an effort by the wife to be supportive of her husband's career and to take some of the pressure off him. Wife after wife told us how family life became much less chaotic when they were able to let a little air out of their high-stress, dual-career lives. Most educated, accomplished women are married to men with demanding careers. By running the show at home, by assuming primary responsibility for the kids, the finances, and the house, these women—the family CEOs—allow their husbands to concentrate more fully on their work and spend more of their free time with their children.

As we got to know these women, we were presented with many surprises. They are not all baby boomers, who might be expected to have traditional leanings. Many are in their twenties and thirties, well-educated with ambitious career goals. They are not necessarily emulating their mothers. Their mothers often worked outside the home. Rather they are women who, for a given period of time, choose to put their families and husbands' careers first. "I love being there to help my husband as he advances in his career. I like knowing that he can go to work and work hard and not have to worry about what's happening to his child or home. He knows that I'll take care of most things and when I need help, I'll ask him for it. I love knowing that I have the power to make our home a wonderful place to be," says Jennifer Boutte, thirty-two, of Smyrna, Georgia.

When Ellen Hart Peña's husband accepted a cabinet post in the first Clinton administration, it meant moving from family-friendly Denver to socially stiff Washington, DC. Why would she agree to do that? "One of the things I admire and respect beyond words is my husband's commitment to public service, and I have encouraged him with that," she says. "He's very good at it and we need people like him. And I'm prepared to make those sacrifices because I think it's important for us and for our kids and for other people."

∾ The Statistics Are on Our Side ∾

Sure, flowers and candy on Valentine's Day is one way of saying "I love you," but doesn't putting our careers on hold truly authenticate the covenant we made when we said, "I do?" We are choosing to do something for our husbands that others may see as foolish, but in our hearts we know is right—for now. We never feel like we are retreating or caving in. We view our decisions with a sense of optimism, believing that when we are ready to return to the workforce, opportunities will be there. In fact, the statistics are in our favor. We are living longer and spending more years in the workforce. Women born in 1960 can expect to live 73.1 years[6] and the average eighteen-year-old who marries can expect to spend twenty-nine years in the workforce.[7]

Many women look to their mothers for inspiration about future possibilities. Lois Voth, forty-three, of Garden City, New York, calls her seventy-four-year-old mother, "my hero." Lois explains: "She raised her children and helped my father on their farm in Kansas. But now she's more active than ever, working in community and church activities. She's intelligent and resourceful. Because of her, I too can see many years of productive work ahead."

Jennifer Boutte has wonderful memories of life with an at-home mom who did it all—at different times. "As we were growing up," Jennifer says, "my mom took a course or two at a time to eventually earn a Ph.D. in sociology. She is now a professor at the University of Texas at Austin and runs a breast cancer screening clinic. She serves on a number of boards and belongs to a number of local and national organizations. She's a dynamic woman, and I learned quite a bit from her, particularly that you can pursue your passions and raise a family without having to do everything at once."

We also feel a sense of entitlement, an empowerment to cut back now and go back later. Candace says, "Women have a greater sense of the length of their lives. They have mothers who are professionals and still working in their sixties. They see Gloria Steinem still running her magazine. We're the first generation that has seen women continuing to advance. If you stay at home, people think you've given up work life. But what's ten years out of your work life?"

It's time to toss away those preconceived notions that women who put their husbands' careers first are weak. Wrong! This is not a decision that can be made by a woman who feels less than equal with her husband. What kind of woman puts her husband's career ahead of her own? New traditional wives have a good—sometimes even great—sense of self. Gail Deutsch, a New York psychiatric social worker, explained how that strong sense of self connects to the decision to assume a more traditional role. "These women are secure enough in who they are that they don't have to prove anything to the world. With good self-esteem, it doesn't bother them," she says.

Let's remember that women who take this bold step aren't declaring war against feminist traditions; they are embracing them. They refuse to be typecast; they will play many roles. And they will not let anyone dictate which role to play or when to play it. It's their choice. Gutsy, brave, not afraid to break new ground—that doesn't sound very conventional to us!

⚲ Giving Up a Really ⚲ Good Career . . . for Now!

"The women's movement means equality of opportunity to do whatever you want to do," says Alison, and she knows of what she speaks. After Princeton, Alison worked her way through law school and won a competitive slot as an associate in a San Francisco law firm. Her husband is also an attorney, and they quickly were caught up in a 24-7 workweek until Alison hit her mid-thirties. She wanted children but realized that something in their frantic lifestyle had to change. "During my years in college and law school, I naively believed all the media hype about working moms, super moms, day care, and so on, and assumed I could do it all at once—career, family, marriage, personal life. And then reality kicked in for me! I had a lot invested in my legal career and did not make the decision to leave lightly. It became clear to us quickly that in order to have any semblance of a marriage relationship, let alone family life when children came along, we both could not continue to work those long hours. Further, we did not wish to have children and 'outsource' our parenting responsibilities to paid help. I personally did not wait to have children in my thirties in order for others to raise them."

Some might criticize Alison's decision and argue that she could have continued to work and let her husband stay home. She counters: "In our marriage, we made the decision for me to stay home based on personal and practical concerns, and not guided by concerns about sexual politics. I was disenchanted with large law firm practice, while Dan enjoyed it. He also had no inclination to stay home with children, while I looked forward to it. Over the years while having three babies, we have learned that a division of labor makes sense and works best for us given Dan's demanding job. Dan does have time and freedom to pursue his career and maximize the income he brings in for the family, while I am the

CEO of the household. If Dan had a much less demanding career, we probably would have been able to work out a more equitable division of household and child-rearing duties."

Alison and Dan started living on one salary even before they had the first of their three boys, so they could get used to a more modest income. In the astronomically priced San Francisco Bay area, where they lived at the time, that was no easy feat. Other women lawyers Alison met confided that they wished they could do the same, but it was not feasible as they were locked into high mortgages, vacations, and expensive family "toys." Alison decided they could live with a smaller house and without cable television and two vacations every year. To her dual-career friends, it looks like Ali is getting the less desirable end of the deal. She vehemently disagrees, "Our marriage is a true partnership built on commitment, in which Dan is currently the chief bread winner and I am the CFO managing the household finances."

Deborah Williams, forty, who has a doctorate in clinical psychology, made a similar choice to back-burner her career for her husband, Herb, the former New York Knick's backup center. On the very day in February 1989 that Deborah was scheduled to sign a contract to enter an Indianapolis psychiatric group practice, her husband was traded from the Indiana Pacers to the Dallas Mavericks. It was then that Deborah decided to back-burner her career for the duration of Herb's stint as a professional basketball player—however long that might be. "I made a commitment to him and he made a commitment to me that we would never part and we have never had to do that," Deborah says. "If I had stayed in Indianapolis and I was in private practice now, I doubt that we'd still be married because Herb is very family oriented. He needs his family around him. He always has."

Don't get the wrong idea. Deborah doesn't say that she can't have a job. "A job, you can take for a while. A career, you can't do that. A career takes a lot of time, a lot of energy, and a lot of investment on your part. You can't just stop on a dime because it can hurt your career more than it can help it."

⚬ Timing Is Everything ⚬

Back-burnering a career is not some one-size-fits-all solution. Alison quit her job in a law firm before she had children. Deborah put her career on hold when her husband moved to a new city. Other women stop working after the first child. Julia Olkin Meza, forty, of Castro Valley, California, took a different approach. Julia, who holds a Ph.D. in mathematical sciences, told us that she always knew she would continue working after having children. She took off about two months after the births of her son and daughter and put them in full-time day care while she returned to her job at the prestigious Stanford Research Institute. When her oldest child was just entering kindergarten, Julia took a new position at another company, a ninety-minute commute each way. "It turned out not to be what I expected," she says. "It was a small company. It sounded great, but the work was not the right match for me. I started in August and that December I decided to take two weeks off at home. It felt great. I decided I didn't want to go back to work. I brought it up to my husband completely out of the blue. I said, 'You're going to be amazed at this: I don't want to work anymore.'

He was shocked and concerned: could we make it on one salary? I did a back-of-the-envelope check and figured we could. I gave my notice, left a week later, and never looked back."

That was in January 1998, and Julia doesn't miss her graphing calculator one bit. "I have no desire to read the mathematical journals I once read," she says. "I don't go to the conferences. I put my degree to use, but now that is not what I want. I've shown that I can do it. I did something I liked; I did it for me."

☙ Well, No Thank You ❧

We discovered that many new traditional wives were highly valued employees and even after they departed, companies sought them out, attempting to lure them back. It's flattering to have an employer dangle a job offer. It takes resolve to remember why we quit in the first place and to realize that we must say no sometimes even to an offer that a part of us would like to accept. From time to time, Alison has been tempted by the possibility of part-time work. A few years ago she was offered a position as a part-time associate, which in a law firm means about thirty-five hours a week. She took out her calculator and tallied the salary less the costs of working—from clothes to child care to prepared meals. The bottom line: $10,000 net. "We'll live on $10,000 less," she said, passing up the job.

It also helps to have a long-range view, bolstered by the self-confidence that there will be other opportunities down the road. Carol Rolnick, forty-seven, from Ellicott City,

Maryland, has a resume that includes some prestigious jobs (director of planning at age twenty-seven for Georgetown University Hospital) as well as some unusual ones (dolphin trainer at the National Aquarium in Baltimore). While teaching dolphins was challenging and fun, Carol also has a husband, who is an emergency-room physician with rotating shifts, two children, and a menagerie of animals, including horses, at their rural Maryland home. Carol decided to quit her job and, at her husband's urging, try her hand at writing novels, a long-delayed dream.

Then one day, out of the blue, a former colleague called and asked her if she was interested in the demanding position as head administrator at a rural Maryland hospital. The job carried a six-figure salary, a chance to jump-start her career, and a lot of headaches and problems. Her husband suggested she take the job, even though it meant moving. He was willing to find another ER position and help with a move to a new house. But Carol declined, remembering that she had quit her other job because she wanted to be the "heart of the house."

There were other reasons, too. "It would have probably torn the family up," she says. "I would have been working ten to twelve hours a day and totally stressed out with the health-care issues facing a small hospital. I would have been a very difficult person to be around." The offer was tempting, and many women like Carol struggle with similar decisions. For Carol, the timing was off; it was too soon. She had tried working full-time and found, even with nannies and other paid help, it just hadn't meshed for her. To every season there is a time, and this is the time for Carol to stay home and explore her writing possibilities. There will be other seasons for work in the fields outside her home.

⚬ Sharing in His Dream ⚬

Part of being a new traditional wife is not only back-burnering your career but also providing the emotional support so your husband can flourish in his career. Certainly that's an against-the-grain notion in these days of gender equality. Julia's husband, Juan, who is also a research mathematician, was recently asked to serve as a consultant with the Department of Energy in Washington, DC, for a full year. Julia urged him to accept the plum assignment, with the promise of frequent visits and e-mail. "This is a superb opportunity for my husband," she says. "He has a chance to actually make a difference, deciding how a big chunk of government money will be spent, having a say in what research gets funded." Julia admits that if she had been working full-time, Juan could have never considered the position. Now she can serve as both mom and surrogate dad (including double-duty as soccer coach) for the twelve months her husband is three thousand miles away. She's counting on her network of family and friends to help her, and planning a summer vacation for herself and the children in (where else?) the nation's capital.

Julia is not alone. We found dozens of remarkable, accomplished women who back-burnered and told their husbands, "Go for it." Case in point: meet Rina Anderson. If Rina were single, a "Strictly Personals" ad in *New York* magazine might read: "Beauty and Brains: attractive, down-to-earth, blue-eyed, blond nonsmoker; holds B.A. in Asian languages and culture and M.B.A. from top East Coast university; worked in Japan translating technical documents related to semiconductors and in New York for major investment banking firm.

Don't be frightened by the resume. Still loves happy hours and knows how to have a good time."

The real Rina Anderson is married and left a plum job at Salomon Smith Barney with a whopping six-figure salary to become, in her own words, "a corporate wife." At thirty-two, Rina is a smart, savvy woman who could punch a considerable hole in the proverbial glass ceiling. But for now, she is choosing a different course, helping her husband of five years, Hitoshi "Tommy" Tomizawa, launch a medical practice treating the Japanese community in L.A. She explains: "His career is much more important. Yes, I want to have a great career. I want to earn my own money. I want to be intellectually challenged. Economically, on Wall Street I had more earning power than he has, but he had a bigger emotional investment in his career. He's been through years of medical school, years of training. I did two years of an M.B.A. He needs me out there."

Make no mistake. Rina is not going out to L.A. to play doctor's wife. Her idea is more along the lines of business partner. She confidently rattles off the details: "He's having to do financial modeling, scenario planning, thinking about marketing, and these are skills he doesn't have. The guys who are going to be the survivors or will come out ahead of this system are the ones who understand business because HMOs have turned health care into a business model. In a traditional health care model, you didn't think about money. Now you think about money."

Concerned about his wife's happiness, Tommy questioned Rina's monumental decision to jump off the fast track for him. "When I told him that I wanted to leave the job and go back to L.A. he said, 'Wait a second now. This isn't paradise here. I'm afraid that you are going to get bored and that you're going to be dissatisfied and you're going to take it out on me.' He really balked and I was hurt. I was like, 'Don't you want me to come back to L.A.?' I'm less afraid because it was my choice. He did not ask to me to do this. It was completely my idea."

When we met Rina, just two days before her move, this confident, accomplished woman admitted to being a bit frightened about her new career path. "I'm afraid that my self-esteem will be chiseled away. I am. It's a fear. I want to do something more nontraditional. I want to look for something I can really do out of the house. I want to spend some time supporting what Tommy's doing. He doesn't have the budget to do all the things that he wants and needs to do, so I want to support him, but I'm also afraid of getting a little bit too drawn into, sort of seduced, by the hospital."

While there is talk of Rina helping out in his office because the tight budget doesn't allow for a support team, she is not sold on the idea. Being a "corporate wife" is one thing. Working side by side is another. She says they live together wonderfully, but traveling together isn't always perfect. Working together? Only time will tell.

Rina was uncertain as to what she would do in L.A. but knows that she will continue as the family financial manager. "I have always been. That's what the norm is in Japan. In Japanese society this is a respected role. It's high status to be a housewife and to be married. To stay at home is very respected in Japan. That's the norm." We reminded Rina that somewhere along the way the standard question is sure to pass someone's lips, "Rina, and what do you do?" Her quick reply, "Well, if he is Japanese, he won't ask."

Clearly, the average husband doesn't accept a yearlong assignment like Julia's or take a permanent job clear across the country like Rina's. But there are many men whose careers demand night and weekend hours and extensive travel. The tales are endless. We all know how difficult it is to go solo to a family wedding or a holiday celebration. These are special moments we want to share with our spouse. "Fred missed both my brothers' weddings because he was working in Mexico in the orchestra," says Cathy Myers, who was 100 percent behind her husband's decision to accept a job as a bassoonist with an orchestra in Toluca, Mexico. "I attended both weddings without him. I would have liked to have him there, but it wasn't really a big deal. It seemed clear that getting this opportunity to play in a major orchestra was extremely important to him and there was no one else to cover his part!"

Some women face this kind of absenteeism on a regular basis because their husbands are not 9-to-5ers. Fathers with the best intentions of getting home on time for a ballet recital or the Little League play-off game are often late or even worse, no-shows. An airport delay, a long conference call, a client from out of town. Unpredictable, yes. Unusual, no.

When we first met Rosanne Breen, she was worried about whether her husband, Mike, would be in town for their son's upcoming first communion. Rosanne, a great organizer with a master's degree in business administration, had everything planned. The only area out of her control was Mike's work schedule. As a sportscaster for the NBA, it was possible that Mike would have to work the day of the communion, announcing a play-off game halfway across the country. "My husband is on pins and needles about it," she says.

Mike's job frequently takes him away from the family. Recognizing that it has taken years of hard work for him to go from announcing on Fordham University's radio station to prime-time television, Rosanne would never put obstacles in his path. She has always known that life with Mike meant long work days and late nights for him, often away from home. But she also knew what she needed for that situation to work: her support system of family and friends nearby. It took some convincing to get Mike to buy a house on Long Island, since he wasn't anxious to live in an area famous for its traffic jams. In retrospect, Rosanne and Mike are both ecstatic with the decision. Rosanne says, "He loves it. He loves the fact that my family is here, and I think that made a big difference for me. Even though he's not around, I have my whole family." Mike may announce the play-by-play, but this time it was Rosanne who made a good call. During the first year in their new house, Mike worked every weekend from August until the following July, making it home only for Thanksgiving and Christmas. Her instinct to be surrounded by her family—Rosanne is one of four children—was right.

Rosanne, like other new traditional wives, sees herself as part of a team—a partnership—and what benefits her husband benefits her and their children. It's a win-win situation. Margo Litzenberg, 26, is another such woman. She supported her husband's decision to become a Navy pilot. She knew full well that it would mean a six-year commitment, that he would be away for six months at a stretch, that even when he was home he would frequently be gone two to four weeks at a time and that she would move across the country several times, away from family in Ohio. Yet she would not have it any other way. "It's such a great opportunity for him.

Sometimes I think that he'd rather be in the plane than with me, but when you find an individual like that, someone who is willing to put his life on the line for his country, how can you not admire that so much? He's a wonderful individual; he's so selfless."

At first, Margo continued to work after her son was born, managing to find positions in California and in Florida as her husband was transferred two times across the country. She confidently carried on with her life as usual when he shipped out on a six-month deployment, leaving her and their two-year-old son alone in northern Florida. Life went smoothly for a few months. She worked at an elementary school, and her son stayed in a nearby day-care center. Then one crisis after another hit. Her son developed a brain inflammation that could call for surgery; her husband's grandmother died in Ohio. Should she have her son undergo surgery? Should she fly home for the funeral? Not only did she need to make these decisions alone, she couldn't even share them with her husband via e-mail or phone because she didn't want to upset him while he was flying dangerous missions in the Persian Gulf.

"The deployment was a really amazing experience for me because at the end I felt I was a very strong person. I can handle anything now because I have developed this coping mechanism. Anytime you go through a problem and look back on what you learned, the hindsight can make you a stronger and better person. My weakness is that I can be a very codependent person. I learned to be independent. I want a T-shirt that says, 'I survived,'" Margo says. As she became more independent, Margo also became more comfortable with her choice not to work. "I became more confident in my decision that I don't have to do anything career oriented right now. This is my thing, being a Navy wife."

How many times have we heard a husband say "I could never do what my wife does"? Margo discovered that handling the home front brought yet another unexpected bonus: "The funny thing is that I think he loves me more now and admires how strong I've become, and he respects me more than ever. He said, 'I don't think I could do what you did.' And he didn't know the half of it: what it's like to care for a two-year-old, twenty-four hours a day by yourself, to handle a screaming, sick child through the night all alone."

While Margo finds increased self-confidence in her ability to handle decisions and crises alone, she constantly emphasizes that her main motivation was to help her husband fulfill his dreams . . . safely. "My involvement with the other [Navy] families helps build a community that's very strong, that helps the wives to be alone and the men to do their jobs. I think he realized that too, and that gives him the security to do his job better. He can fly safer knowing also that there are twenty-nine other wives who will take care of me if I need it. I feel I made the right decision [not to work]: My husband is happier, I am happier, the whole family is happier."

๑ Circles of Friends ๑

Forget *mano a mano*; sisterhood is where it's at. From the Ya-Yas to groups for clergy wives, girl talk is back, stamped an official trend by *The New York Times*.[8] Fortunately, support groups have finally shed the stigma of being only for the dysfunctional, because even healthy women find comfort listening to other women who face similar conflicts, changes, and choices. Who can better understand your feelings—the ups and downs, the delight and disappointment—than someone going through something similar?

For many women, it is validating to find out that there are other smart women at home; every interesting, intelligent woman in the United States is not in an office somewhere. "I was surprised at the education level of women in my mother's group in Princeton, New Jersey," says Lila Lawler, thirty-six, now living in Riva, Maryland. "There was a lawyer and a Ph.D. student. Yes, we talked about baby stuff, but the conversation went on to other topics."

Many wives find themselves home alone at dinner and bath time while their husbands work late or travel for business. Not only are the babies beset by what Dr. Spock called "evening irritability," mothers are too. Lois Voth discovered that sharing evening meals and bath routines with her women friends was one way to handle that problem. As a thirty-something mother of a one-year-old in Dallas, she found four other mothers, all with children the same age, whose husbands were rarely home at bedtime. So, many nights they all met at one house, fed and bathed the children, and returned home with the kiddies in their pajamas, ready for bed. "They were all interesting, very intelligent, gifted women," recalls Lois. "It was wonderful to share those routines together instead of doing them alone. Also important was that we shared information about parenting. It was incredibly reassuring to know that it was as challenging for them as it was for me." When she moved to Virginia a few years later, Lois sought out other comrades in arms and they too often shared the evening routines. "Those friends served as my lifeline.

They could understand the life I was living because they were doing the same exact things," she says.

A support group may be as informal as walking with other women every morning for both exercise and venting. It can be meeting with an encouraging group of women writers who are trying their hand at fiction. Perhaps circles of friends are most crucial to women whose husbands' jobs are especially stressful or hazardous. The wives of police officers and firefighters immediately understand each other's feelings and fears. Imagine women whose husbands have dangerous jobs and are away for six months at a stretch. For them, a support group is not an option, it's necessary for survival.

As a military wife, Margo joined a Navy wives' club. Belonging to a club to attend social events is one thing but to call on the women for emotional support, Margo had to make the time to form friendships with the women, and her work schedule just didn't give her that flexibility. Emotional ties are not built on a quick hello at the grocery store. Those connections come after hours at the playground, volunteering at the preschool, sharing a peanut butter lunch with other mothers and kids on a rainy day, helping with a community project. For five months Margo debated the decision to leave work, playing out all the familiar arguments in her head. She says, "I did lots of thinking about how could I do the career, support my husband, stay away from my son while at work, and still be happy. It really was a self-esteem issue because for women of the '90s the main role model is to be a career mom, but I realized that this is not working for me. I was emotionally overwhelmed. I have no family down here. The only support is the wives' club, and if I don't reach out and be there for other wives when they need help, I won't be able to get that back when I need it. I need that support when he's gone."

Margo speaks from her heart: "The support group I have of military wives isn't just necessary for me to stay positive mentally, it is actually essential to my life. Without other wives to speak to who experience what we do, I am not sure I could survive. That sounds melodramatic, I know, but ultimately it is what I believe. I have plenty of friends from college and all other walks of life who just really can't comprehend what my life is like. With the wives of military men, there is an instant bond, complete understanding for what life is about for us. Then there is always the thought that if something would ever happen to my husband, I know that group of women would be the ones holding me up all along the way. These wives are my lifeline. They hold me together when I am just too exhausted to move and feel like I just can't make it another day separated from my husband. They listen and understand my pain as they feel it too. They know how it feels to hold a child and tell him 'Daddy loves you and he'll be home soon,' even though you still have four more months to go. I can't imagine not having these amazing women to hold onto for they bring more strength, love, and courage into my life than I can even explain."

The other Navy wives helped her navigate the difficult decisions during those months her husband was away, and the self-esteem that she worried about losing actually blossomed. The experience was like a do-it-yourself Outward Bound. Wives, military or otherwise, don't need a packaged outdoor experience to help build faith in one's self; just give them an old-fashioned crisis or two and chances are, they will make it through with flying colors, emerging more self-confident.

𐅻 Retooling Your Skills 𐅻
for a New Stage

Making the culturally incorrect choice to go against the grain is certainly difficult, and the impact of that decision reverberates for years. So how do we live with its consequences? Actually, all it takes is a shift in the way we look at life and its possibilities. We find that by seeking a new paradigm—by viewing life from a slightly different angle—we are presented with exciting, unforeseen opportunities for personal and professional growth.

"Retooling" is our catch-all phrase for how the new traditional wife thinks out of the box. Retooling simply means using old skills in new ways, both in the home and in the workplace. In other words, if you have it, use it. Women retool those hard-won skills into meaningful work that fits their lives as wives and mothers. While the definition of retooling may be short, its usage could fill pages and pages.

From coast to coast, women find creative ways to nourish their individuality and talents at different times. For some, this means volunteer work or part-time work; others opt for flextime. A lawyer who now uses her legal talents to draw up a document on computer usage and restrictions for her children's school is retooling. A professional planner who learns about marketing and advertising so she can work part-time from home for a family business is retooling. A banker who goes back to school to get a nursing degree is retooling. A teacher who reenters education after sixteen years at home and rises quickly to become a principal is retooling. A journalist who coauthors with her father a memoir of his youth in Nazi Germany is retooling. While the family CEO makes her husband and children the priority in her life, that doesn't mean that she ignores an integral part of herself: her desire for fulfilling work.

Retooling is not always planned in advance. Sure, some women in their twenties look far off into the future and say "I want a husband and children and time at home" and make plans accordingly. Some sock away extra money; others make adjustments in their careers, cut back their hours, or find more flexible work. Most of us wing it, adopting the plan-as-you-go mode. Whether it's long-term or on-the-spot planning, women are driven by a sense of time, both present and future. Life seems to whiz by at hyperspeed. Many women suddenly realize that being thirty-five with a hard-working husband and two kids is not going to happen again, so why not spend five or ten years at home? "If I can die saying I gave 10 percent of my life to my small children to get them grounded and feeling loved, then I'll consider myself successful," says Candace, who has developed web sites as a volunteer for three groups.

Women are retooling every day without even knowing it. While holding down the home front, the new traditional wife hones skills such as organization, flexibility, problem solving, and communication that are valued in the working world. What woman hasn't used these skills for anything from whipping up a last-minute dinner to getting the hot-water heater fixed, from helping with homework to refinancing the mortgage? Often women do it all at the same time! Heidi Brennan, a former management training consultant and career counselor, calls this expertise that translates to the marketplace "transcendent work skills." She now works part-time as policy director for Mothers at Home, a national non-profit organization based near Washington DC, whose monthly publication, *Welcome Home,* reaches thirty thousand readers. "Mothers at home develop what I call 'human Valium' because of their ability to be patient and handle stress. It's stressful to handle a three-year-old's temper tantrum. In my work days I saw a lot of forty-year-olds' temper tantrums. I think I could handle them a lot better now."

Ellen Gordon retooled using her "transcendent work skills" after many years as an at-home mom. This president and chief operating officer of Tootsie Roll Industries in Chicago told *USA Today* that motherhood prepared her for her job. "It makes you very efficient with time," she said. "You've got to send them off to school and your husband to work. It's like when you're an executive. You're directing people."[9]

Nina Salkin, the wife of a rabbi, could serve as the prototype for retooling. By any standard, Nina is an accomplished woman. As associate creative director at a leading New York City advertising agency, Nina planned ad campaigns for corporations from Colgate to Kal Kan. Her client list read like the *Fortune* 500. When Nina moved from New York City to be with her husband in Doylestown, Pennsylvania, she took a job that didn't last very long at an industrial ad agency. "They had clients that made widgets, literally, and I had come out of consumer advertising," she says. The clients may not have been a good fit, but the company was on the cutting edge of using computers. Never one to pass up an opportunity to learn something new, Nina leaped at the chance to work with computers, which she calls "a crucial tool in my life." Today Nina has retooled by using those same creative talents and computer skills for community work. Good Seasons and Pine Sol can't count on her for copy, but thousands of rabbis' spouses around the world look forward to her biannual

SpouseConnection, the newsletter she edits and designs on her computer. Like her top-notch ad campaigns, she writes copy that is interesting and lively, candidly addressing issues relevant to rabbis' spouses. And with the same energy that she once used to launch ad campaigns, Nina recently put together a weeklong study of Israel for her youngest son's elementary school. "I'm just trying to take the skills that I had and use them in different areas," Nina told us. "We did a whole week of Israel studies. We built an archaeological dig, and we built Shouk and Bedouin tents. We did learning stations in the library. I got paid a lot of money to write little ditties about dog food, but they don't pay me to do what I just did for Manorhaven School. I did it because it was important to me."

As each year passes, Nina's contribution to her community grows. There is no more commuting; there are no more whirlwind cross-country business trips. Still Nina reaches deep within herself to bring creativity and intelligence to all her important projects, whether she is working hands-on with schoolchildren or at a meeting for Child Abuse Prevention Services, where she is a trustee. Nina's gifts are by no means wasted; rather, they are merely retooled.

Two New York sisters took contrasting approaches to retooling their careers. Bernadette Cain planned as she went along from single to married to two children. After the birth of her second child, she quit her fascinating but stressful job managing a psychiatry practice at a large hospital and began looking for a career path that would give her more flexibility. She went back to school evenings and weekends and slowly earned an M.B.A. As her children got older, she took on several small consulting jobs with health-care organizations. Over six years of sporadic work, she built her resume to the point where she was hired to manage an office for ten pediatricians, five minutes from her home. Her deal: no more than twenty hours a week. "My mantra now is balance," she says. "Over that decade all those courses and little jobs added up to enough experience to qualify me for the perfect job." Bernadette's sister, Dot Whalen, took the long-range approach. An orthodontist, she bought her first house with a home office so she could be close to her two small boys. Although she could have worked more, she kept her schedule to three days a week. Even though her boys are now in high school and college, she has resisted the temptation to expand her practice. That's part of her plan too. "For years I worked part-time so I could have the time for my family. Now it's my turn, and those two days 'off' are for me," she says.

As we talked with women about how they retooled, we found that their approach fell into one of four areas. The first is empowerment. Women feel empowered to move in and out of the workforce. We walk away from our careers because we have confidence that a job—though maybe not the same one—will be there when we want to return. The second is exploration. Many women use the time that their careers are on hold as "fishing expeditions" in which they find new ways to sharpen old skills or to explore uncharted waters. The third and fourth areas—working for others or ourselves—are the payoff. For some of us, it's employment—part-time, full-time, flextime. For others, it's becoming an entrepreneur, starting an exciting new business and being able to say, "I'm the boss."

Let's take a closer look now at how women incorporate empowerment, exploration, employment, and entrepreneurship into their lives.

⚬ Embracing the Power ⚬

Few traditional wives who step off the career track for a while are by no means worried that returning to work could pose a problem. In fact, most show little concern; they have a sense of entitlement. Unlike the generation before them whose mothers said "Become a teacher; you can always go back to it," this new generation of women feel entitled to return to any job, profession, or career—if and when they choose. Maybe it's the years of training and the decade on the job. Or maybe it's the big bucks invested in an education that gives them this sense of empowerment. With square shoulders and heads held high, these women say, "Something will be there for me when I make the decision to return." "Look at Madeleine Albright," they say, or "what about Sandra Day O'Connor?" We do have great role models. The naysayers ask, "Aren't they being naive?" While this question will certainly be answered in the early decades of this new millennium, all bets are in our favor because many of us have been proactive, knowing that returning is a good possibility. We have been taking courses, teaching courses, expanding our contacts, subscribing to trade magazines, going to meetings with people from our field, and keeping up in all sorts of ways. It's not as if we are simply snapping our fingers and saying, "Okay, take me back."

When Rina left her equity research job in New York City to be with her husband Tommy in L.A., there was never a doubt in her mind that she could reenter the working world whenever and wherever she pleased thanks to her impressive and interesting resume. Without missing a beat she began day trading on the Internet and studying for the Certified Financial Analyst Level 1 Exam.

We intended to call Rina to find out how she was doing but she got to us first. "Trading has been going well, so I wanted to get a part-time or temporary job to earn money to add to my trading account. When I started looking on the Internet, one click led to another and I found this analyst position for a Japanese-speaking M.B.A. at Universal to help with planning for the opening of the Osaka theme park. It sounded tailor-made for me, so I had to go for it. It's more responsibility than I was originally looking for, but since it seems like such an interesting job, I couldn't pass it up. I guess I'm not eligible to be in your book," she ended apologetically. To the contrary, Rina, you have just proven our point!

While Rina embraced a sense of empowerment about jumping back into the world of finance, Kathy Scheller, forty-seven, felt empowered to leap into an entirely new arena. When the youngest of her three sons started school, so did she. Kathy had ended a successful twelve-year career as a banker with the birth of her second son. As her boys went off to school, she could have found a part-time job in one of the corporate headquarters in nearby Stamford, Connecticut. Instead, she chose to fulfill a personal dream. "When I was about thirty years old a light bulb went on," she says. "One day I realized here I was in a bank branch office when I'd really rather be working in medicine. I looked down at the ring on my finger and realized I could spend the next twelve years in medical school or having children. The choice was obvious. You can't start children in your forties. So I back-burnered the medical career, but the expectation was that I would get into something medical someday." So at age forty-two, Kathy jumped head first into what she calls the "roaring river" of physiology and anatomy classes in the nursing program at a local college. It took five years to get through the basic science courses—with a straight A average. Kathy's personal reward has been an incredible feeling of accomplishment. "I never pushed myself so hard and put the bar so high," she says. "School is my Prozac!"

Kathy plans to accelerate her classes and finish the last two years on schedule. The reaction of her family is somewhat mixed. Her boys, aged eight, twelve, and fourteen, don't understand why anyone would go to school voluntarily. And what about her husband? "It makes for such a better marriage because school makes me happier on all fronts," she says.

The career of Joan Waldman, forty-seven, of Roslyn, New York, has been like a seesaw. If you had asked Joan as a young woman, "Will you go back to work after you raise your children?" she would have said, "Never." Growing up, she expected to be a stay-home mom. Then after her first teaching job in a nearby town, she thought she'd never leave teaching— that is, until she had two sons, three years apart. Joan and her husband, Larry, decided that raising children was "not a part-time job," so she quit her beloved teaching position. As her boys grew, the idea of going back to teaching was always on the back burner. When she sent her boys off to school each September, she often said, "It should be me going back to work, but I'll wait one more year. I'll play one more tennis game and have lunch a little bit more." Finally, when her boys were both in high school, some sixteen years after she left the classroom, Joan told Larry, "There is no reason why I can't put this whole package together." Friends laughed at her sense of entitlement. "Do you think that the day you decide you want to go back they will hire you?" she was often asked. Happy ending: She *was* hired after a sixteen-year hiatus. Filled with such drive and creative energy, she worked her way up from math support teacher to elementary school principal in just six years.

Like other new traditional wives, Joan was not sitting idle. She served on "every school committee" and was deeply involved in her children's education, even going for special training in a new math curriculum. Her husband was president of their hometown school board for ten years, so Joan became intimately involved with all the controversies. And she kept her connections alive in the school district where she formerly taught, particularly with colleagues including one teacher who had become a school principal. When suddenly one August day a math support slot opened, the contacts and the courses she had taken to help her sons paid off. Joan admits it sounds simpler than it was. "I had been gone for sixteen years, and of course they looked at me like 'Who are you?' I had a lot of nerve walking back in and expecting somebody to hire me. So I certainly did have to prove myself. I felt from day one that I had to make a statement that I was worthy of having been hired after sixteen years of not working. The fact that they gave me a job—it was luck. I was here at the right moment. I had the right people pushing for me."

Once she was back with the chalk in her hand, she realized how much she loved being in the classroom. Her boys, aged thirteen and sixteen, were not as elated. "Literally overnight I told my family that I was going back to work," she says. "And my children looked at me and told me that they didn't want to be latchkey children. And I told them at their age they would be called latchkey adults. My family will say now that this is the best thing that I ever did and that I did it at the perfect time."

"If I could only do it again" or "I would do it better now" are thoughts we have all had at some time. Joan had those thoughts too. "I used to say I should go back and be a teacher because I could do this really well now," she says. "Life experience is the key. I know what's correct and what's not correct. I feel like I've raised my own children and now I'm raising everybody else's here. I want for them what I got for my own. That's my job. It's in my heart."

❦ Life in an Exploratorium ❦

We may not have a term that accurately describes us—the women who put our careers on hold for the sake of our husbands and children—but there sure is a lot of name calling going on. We've gone from "ladies who lunch" to "stay-at-home moms." Now it's time to set the record straight. Many of us don't have time for luncheons—yogurt in the car?—and we are never at home. Let's talk about how much we are really doing and how multitasked we really are. Think about what we do while we are watching TV. Fold the laundry. Make to-do lists. Read the paper. Clip coupons. The list goes on. This unique ability to focus on more than one thing at a time is why so many women are able to take care of their families, do part-time work, volunteer, and still find time to explore new interests that later can parlay into new careers.

With a sense of the ephemeral nature of time, women use their years at home for experimentation and evaluation, often discovering new skills and interests. Whether these high energy women decide to work full-time or part-time, when they feel the time is right to reenter the workforce, they don't just wet their big toe, they dive in headfirst—and not necessarily into the same old pool. "I consider my time at home an experiment with my career. I am comfortable with the chaos of change and confident it will sort itself out," says Heidi Brennan, a former management consultant and career counselor. Like many other women, she made the transition from one career to the other by looking at both her skills and interests. She explains, "Skill assessment is one aspect of career planning and interest assessment is the other. But they are both ongoing processes. I knew what my skills were, but motherhood added new interests. Until I had children and committed myself to being at home I couldn't foresee the new possibilities in my life."

Joanne Brundage, forty-seven, calls exploration "the best-kept secret about staying home." Joanne, of Elmhurst, Illinois, worked as a postal carrier until her second child was born when she quit her job to stay at home. But after a few months Joanne decided that there must be others out there just like her so she placed an advertisement in a local paper. Soon her living room was filled with women. From that 1987 meeting sprang an organization called FEMALE (Formerly Employed Mothers at the Leading Edge) that now numbers 6,500 members in 170 chapters nationwide. Talk about exploring new areas! Joanne is now the executive director involved in all aspects of planning and policy. "Being at home gives you a second chance to prioritize and decide what you want to do with your future, and not be caught up in the same mind-set as you were in your twenties when you never even considered kids or changing jobs."

FEMALE recently did a survey of its members and found that more than 70 percent plan to return to work in the future. Of those planning to reenter the workforce, more than one-third do not plan to return to the same occupation and another third are undecided.

"Down time" at home can be daunting, especially for women who have spent the last decade with their lives scheduled to the minute. As we get beyond what one mother dubbed "the basic survival mode" and slowly adopt a new rhythm (punctuated by a predictable routine), we begin to look beyond the four walls and wonder what else might be out there that can fit into our new lives. Alison Carlson's future might include law, but she's not sure. Right now she's experimenting. "Being at home gives one the time to try things out, even if it is just squeezed into the small, spare moments of life at home. Had I been working full- or part-time, I wouldn't have had the freedom to experiment or develop something that is just right for me. As my children get older, I expect that I will have more time to devote to pursuing a vocation of my own creation."

Patty Larson, a Chicagoan who worked until age thirty-seven, recalls a conversation with a girlfriend who had just quit her job to stay home with a one-year-old. "My friend said she will never go back to work. But last week, while watching her son toddle everywhere and get into everything, she gave me this look and said, 'Is this all there is?'"

Patty, the mother of a preschooler, gave a thoughtful answer to her friend: "I assume this is all there is to life *now*. So I guess it depends on your outlook on life. Do you just 'accept' what you have, or do you enjoy what you have yet try to grab more for yourself? Taking time off to care for children allows us time to really think about what makes us happy and what we want. My jobs have never allowed me to be creative. I just know there is some creativity bottled up inside of me." Although it's not exactly the creative writing she had in mind, Patty edits a quarterly newsletter for a local company and in the process has learned desktop publishing, a skill she hopes will make her more marketable some day.

When Loretta was a few years away from having an empty nest, she knew that it was time to revisit dusty old plans to get a master's degree, which she had put on hold decades earlier. Flipping through New York University's catalog, she discovered an unusual program, a master's degree in liberal studies. "I felt like it was made just for me. It had my name on it. I could take courses in a number of departments as well as interdisciplinary courses designed specifically for liberal studies students. Sure it took me a little longer, but hey, who cares. It was for me, no one else, and I loved every minute of it. As graduation approached, I asked myself the question, 'What will I do now?' I felt a whole lot smarter, but a liberal studies degree isn't vocational training. Happily, I had taken a few journalism courses and reconfirmed my passion for writing. In 1992, as I was awarded one degree, I began working toward another, a second master's, this time in journalism. This degree would help me get a job.

"In May 1994, I celebrated my fiftieth birthday and received my second master's degree. Since I started a new career later than most, I felt like I had to move full-speed ahead. Between freelance work and taking a job as special correspondent for *Live,* an entertainment magazine, I was pumping out articles faster than you can say 'clip' and my portfolio swelled.

"If anyone had asked me ten years ago whether I would have a career as a working journalist, a quizzical expression would have been my answer, probably followed by 'Are you nuts?' Today I feel blessed. I have found something exciting and challenging and stimulating to do at the time that I feel is my turn, my time."

Writing was also where Carol Rolnick, forty-seven, found her second career. Carol quit her job as a dolphin trainer in 1993. At first, exhausted from her long hours and juggling, she was content to just take care of her family. "I didn't have any issues of ego or loss of stature when I stopped working because at an early age I hit the top rung," she says. But after a few weeks, Carol began to itch to do something, some kind of work, even if it was only for a few hours a week. Praised by her teachers as a "good writer," she realized that her time at home was the perfect opportunity to stretch her creative muscle. Carol joined a writers' group and set a goal to write every day, and she did—usually for just an hour or two, occasionally for a twelve-hour stretch. "I'd sit there and write and completely forget about dinner," she says. She worked on two manuscripts, both psychological suspense novels.

Sometimes success comes where we least expect it, as it did for Carol. She and two friends were talking about books one night, commenting on the success of some gift books. The conversation drifted on to the "wonderful and wacky" things about the city of Baltimore. And suddenly, as if they were zapped by the wand of a good fairy, the trio decided to write an offbeat guide to Baltimore that visitors could buy for reference and locals for gifts. The result is a recently published guidebook, *Wish You Were Here: A Guide to Baltimore City for Natives and Newcomers,* filled with information on the city's culture, characters, and cuisine.

"I am proud of the Baltimore book and the work that went into it," Carol says. "We were very scrupulous in our research. When it was finally done, there was a tremendous sense of accomplishment and relief. I wanted to sleep for the next month." She continues work on her novels, but the guidebook opened her eyes to new possibilities and, true to form, Carol has a plan. If in two years she doesn't sell a novel, she will turn her attention full-time to travel writing. At that time she will have two children ready to enter college, one right after the other. She also wants to relieve some of the financial pressure on her husband who works long, hectic hours in an inner-city emergency room. Like other new traditional wives, the sense of partnership continues, and often strengthens, as the children grow. "I would like to be earning something and have a sense of pulling my own weight, especially to help a little financially. But whatever I do, writing has become a permanent part of my life," Carol says.

When Connie Sargent, of Brooklyn, New York, began exploring new territory while her career was on hold, she too reaped unexpected dividends. Connie, a former marketing executive with a graduate degree in business, discovered her creative side. "I think, for me, having kids and taking a break allowed me to redefine myself and create a new identity that has nothing to do with my job. I found out all these different things; it's been amazing. I found I have a business degree, but I'm actually a creative person. I took some photography classes. Now I'm into these Polaroid photos and I do pastels with them. It's been great. There's this whole other part of me that I got to know. So when people ask 'What do you do?' I could say, 'I'm an artist.'"

An epiphany came at her children's Quaker school, where Connie wrote a strategic plan and chaired a spiritual committee. Connie realized that when she returns to work, it will not necessarily be in advertising or marketing. "If I'm going to turn my family upside down, I'm going to do something meaningful," she says.

The time at home has also allowed Lois Voth to go in directions she never expected. With a master's degree in educational psychology, she had worked as a therapist in Seattle but stopped because of frequent moves due to her husband's job and raising two children. Two years ago, she first volunteered as a reading assistant at her daughter's school. As a result, she was offered a paid paraprofessional position in the school, which works for her lifestyle right now. It's also been a chance to preview teaching as a possible career down the road. "This part-time job is helping me to gear up and make decisions as to which way to go when I am ready to work more," says Lois. "The idea of teaching always has been in the back of my mind, so this is a good way to see whether I like it and get some feedback on whether I am good at it."

For Kathi Morse, fifty, a meaningful career evolved from volunteer work she did during the years she was an at-home wife and mom in Locust Valley, New York. Growing up in Muncie, Indiana, Kathi had never even heard of social work, let alone considered it as a career. Instead, she followed what was then considered a glamorous career path and became a flight attendant for eight years. After the birth of her first child in 1976, Kathi stayed home. Always regretting she never went to college, she took one course at a time from 1977 until 1994. As her three children grew and she had more time, she became very active in her local Junior League, a service organization that's a lot more serious and substantial than its ladies-who-lunch image. Kathi's volunteer efforts included working with foster children in Family Court and lecturing at local schools on child abuse. "My participation in Junior League helped build my self-esteem and self-confidence. It's the one place where you can stretch yourself and if you fail, they say, 'Okay, let's try it another way,'" says Kathi. "I felt capable and that I made a difference in the lives of people beyond my family. I'm sure I would have never ended up in social work without this volunteer experience."

The semester before her college graduation, at age forty-three, Kathi decided to press on and get her master's degree in social work, going full-time over two years. It was a radical change for her now teenaged children who were used to Mom doing everything, but they and her "very traditional" husband pitched in to relieve some of the household pressures. Kathi now works with children as a bereavement counselor and in a learning disabilities program. Her life has been a series of choices, and she still feels there are more challenges ahead. "Many little pieces are added to the whole as we move through life," she says. "Those pieces keep changing the picture, which encourages or discourages on an ongoing basis. We can keep changing the picture and have it grow from a thumbnail sketch to a mural. My criteria has been asking when I wake in the morning and look in the mirror, do I like who I see and, no matter what happens, can I live with my choices and the possible consequences? If I do and I can, it is good. I am flexible and my mural is an ongoing work."

⁓ Diving into the Digital Age ⁓

The time is variable—it could be midnight or 5:00 A.M.—but the scene is the same: a computer screen blinks in the dark. In front of the screen sits a woman, dressed casually, maybe even in her nightgown, clicking and typing away. The Internet has become the greatest invention since the portable phone for allowing stay-home wives to connect with the outside world for everything from grocery shopping and investment research to finding volunteer and paid work. Most important, being web-savvy develops new skills. Candace Hill has used the Internet to teach research skills to second graders in Evanston, Illinois. That experience opened up other possibilities for her. "I can certainly see developing a career in the schools working with teachers, children, and parents on using the resources of the Internet. Just one idea I had was to open the school's computers in the evening so that low-income families could file their taxes over the Internet," she says.

Industrial psychologist Karen Slora, of Palatine, Illinois, sees the Internet as a way to "keep a hand in" while she's not working full-time. Karen, forty-three, who has a Ph.D. says, "In my previous job, I used the computer for data analysis, but the technology is changing so much that I knew I would need to stay active with computer upgrades if I ever wanted to consider resuming my career. Toward this end, I have put up the first web site for the local chapter of FEMALE. Also, I am doing volunteer survey work for FEMALE, so I have refined my data analysis skills using spreadsheet technology."

The computer makes it possible for countless women to stay wired to an office, part-time and on their terms. Kristi

Hartwell, thirty-four, of Arlington Heights, Illinois, worked full-time for nine years as a manufacturing engineer. She had planned to stop working completely with the birth of her first child. Then it occurred to her to try out a part-time arrangement. "I approached my boss with the idea of working from home," she says. "Everyone was very agreeable about it, and it has turned out to be the best possible choice, in my opinion."

For the past two years, she has used e-mail to stay connected to her coworkers, going into the office just one day a week. Although the new arrangement meant she had to step down from a managerial position, there have been other rewards. Kristi says: "I feel more connected to my family than I think I would have if I worked full time. Staying home has allowed me to embrace my role as mother and to enjoy the job of child rearing without the additional pressure of a full-time job. I give my husband peace of mind about our daughter's care. I have adapted to the freedom I have to arrange my schedule any way I want it. For example, if I want to take my daughter to the park in the morning when it's cool, then I do, and I work a little later in the evening."

Part-time work was also the answer for Marla Cartwright when her career plans were changed by her husband's promotion. Marla, thirty-five, of Murfreesboro, Tennessee, had it all mapped out before she even gave birth: She and her husband, both journalists, would shift their work hours so one parent was always home. A promotion with fixed hours for her husband changed the arrangement so Marla opted to find part-time work. Her writing background qualified her for freelance writing assignments as well as an adjunct position at a local university where she now teaches evening classes. "I was thirty-three when I had my first child so I had a good sense of my skills and my ability to be a wage earner," says Marla, the mother of two little girls. "I was confident that through my contacts I could find freelance jobs. Part-time work can be an ideal arrangement, especially if you position yourself in a career that gives you the flexibility to go into different areas."

Like so many other women, Marla has also found that the Internet provides new areas to explore. As a community moderator for iVillage.com, she manages an online staff of forty-four volunteers and oversees the message boards and chats for iVillage's pets channel. "The payoff is that I have a cheerful, calm toddler and baby and incredible flexibility in my work," she says. "Day care, of any form, was never a remote consideration for our family. And now that I see, firsthand, how they benefit incredibly by having me at home, it's a completely zero option."

We expect that more and more women will find that shopping, surfing, and homework help aside, the computer will allow them to customize work to fit their lives.

ᵔ Finding Work That Works ᵔ

While some women like Connie use the time that they have set aside for their husbands and families to explore new areas of interests, others return to the workforce, but on their own terms, which often translates to part-time employment. In fact, women make up 50 percent of the contingent workforce, which, according to the Bureau of Labor Statistics, includes temporary workers and part-timers. Many women look for jobs with flexible or fewer hours or work they can do from their homes. They retool their original job or profession into something that works better for them now.

"In my search for a part-time job with few hours and lots of money, I discovered that I can teach English as a Second Language. (I am certified to teach English at the secondary level already.) This has opened up a new area that I never would have explored had I not stayed at home," says Jennifer Ransdell, thirty-four, of Chicago. "Teaching people a necessary skill for survival in America is very challenging and rewarding. It has the added benefit of making me more marketable when I am ready to go back to work. All this and I work only five hours a week."

Other women have devised strategies to find suitable part-time work. "When I approached earning an income from the perspective that it *must* be part-time and I *must* be able to do all or most of it at home, it was easier for me to turn away from the lure of an annual salary," says Janet Katz, thirty-three, of Austin, Texas. "I write for a PR firm ten to twelve hours per week, mostly from my home office, but I do spend about five to six hours in their offices. It works very well for me, and I am lucky to have this arrangement."

Punching Your Own Time Clock

Vicky Austin, forty-two, mother of three daughters, ages seven, five and two, tried all of the options—part-time, flextime, and at-home work. After receiving an undergraduate degree from Wellesley, she worked in catering and hotel service management at both the Fairmont and Four Seasons hotels in San Francisco. Realizing that the irregular, long hours and the "immediacy of the restaurant business didn't work for family life," Vicky changed gears. "I had a midlife crisis early . . . at thirty-one," says Vicky, who luckily found a quick fix.

Detecting a market niche and living a stone's throw from Silicon Valley, she decided to get a job writing training manuals and documentation for computer applications for the hospitality industry. When her first child was born, she was still not ready to just walk away from the workplace and decided that working four days a week for a software company would be her panacea. But when her second daughter arrived, nineteen months after her first, she downshifted again. Giving up her four-day-a-week job might have really strapped Vicky's family financially if she hadn't thought ahead and socked away $10,000 in anticipation of losing the family's second income. "As it turned out, we didn't spend the money as staying home was more economical than we thought," she says.

Vicky improvised and found a way to offset some of the income loss: She now teaches classes on technology applications in the hospitality industry in the hotel and restaurant department at City College of San Francisco. "The academic schedule is very appealing. I have summers off," says Vicky, who was not willing to forgo her family's month-long summer vacation at a relative's home in New Hampshire. Vicky continues to mix her personal and professional interests. "With the computer industry, you have to be pretty aggressive because it changes so fast," she says, so she belongs to a women and technology group and chairs the technical committee for her local PTA. When her children's school recently needed to upgrade their computers, Vicky was in charge—from purchasing to installing. "I was the only one who understood the big picture, so I helped decide what to buy and then I literally wired the classes, pulling cable." To us, that's the year 2000 version of doing it all.

Vicky took a plan-ahead approach, reflecting her analytical personality. Vivien Orbach Smith, forty-seven, who lives in the rolling hills of Wilton, Connecticut, chose the more risky plan-as-you-go route. Vivien is a wife and the mother of three children, and her identity as a writer and observant Jew are integral parts of her life. How does she blend all those aspects into a workable lifestyle? Like most other women, she just assumed she'd continue writing, even having visions of delivering her first baby and plugging in the electric typewriter on the hospital tray. We can all smile at that picture, because most of us have had similar delusional thoughts. One baby and then another brought the writing career to a temporary halt. Vivien settled into a happy, friend-and-family-filled at-home life. But something nagged at her from time to time. "I did feel twinges of guilt and embarrassment that I wasn't a working writer," she says. "I felt like I was a hypocrite who had espoused all these feminist ideologies before, wanting equality in everything . . . but very quick to dump my role as one of the two wage earners in our new family."

To at least scratch her creative itch, she volunteered—editing her synagogue's bulletin, doing public relations writing for the children's nursery school, helping friends with business letters, resumes, and speeches, and composing funny toasts and rhyming roasts for birthdays and bar mitzvahs. Her writing and speaking talents caught the attention of a local rabbi who asked her to teach religious school on Sunday mornings and a weekday afternoon to their hardest-to-reach age group: seventh grade and up. "This began a decade of deeply satisfying relationships with adolescents in this community as a teacher and a mentor," she says.

Like many of us, Vivien managed to patch together a part-time job, volunteer work, and tending to her family. Still, she desperately wanted to write. She explains: "Once, while listening to the cast album of *A Chorus Line*, I burst into tears. It wasn't just that I was flashing on being young and determined to write the Great American Novel. It was when one of the young hopefuls sang, 'I'm a dancer ... a dancer dances!' Well, I had to face an unpleasant truth: a writer writes. And maybe other people thought highly of my little ditties and press releases. But I knew what I was really capable of. I was no writer ... I didn't write! The identity I had built for myself was a sham. And that hurt."

But by keeping her writing muscle flexed (albeit with press releases), Vivien was ready for the next step when she heard that a national women's magazine, *Women's World*, was looking for writers. She passed the "tryout" and became a regular contributor, doing phone interviews, often at night when her family was asleep—perfect for her insomniac lifestyle. "I became what I called their *tsuris* (the Yiddish word for "troubles") reporter. I loved talking to women from all walks of life and hearing their stories. Here was a writing job that paid well, and I wouldn't even have to leave the house. My passion for these extraordinary stories refueled my passion for writing."

Vivien, almost without realizing it, was building a writing career layer by layer. No, not strategically planned, but that didn't really matter. What did matter is that it built her confidence, so she was ready for the biggest challenge of her career: helping craft her father's life story. Vivien's dad approached her one day with a manila envelope filled with almost seven hundred pages of a memoir. This was no ordinary memoir. Her father, a survivor of Auschwitz and Buchenwald, had written of his youth hiding in Berlin to avoid detection by the Nazis—sort of an "Anne Frank flees the attic and takes to the streets" story. Not only did the story contain deeply personal recollections that Vivien wasn't sure she really wanted to know about, but it also was written in a colorful, intense, unpublishable prose that was somewhere between German and English. Her father wanted Vivien to edit it. She did more than edit it. Hiring a mother's helper, she spent one summer on research and an exhaustive rewrite. The next summer she put the put the final touches on the book that would become *Soaring Underground: A Young Fugitive's Life in Nazi Berlin*.

The rave reviews the book received prove to Vivien that "I was, in fact, a gifted writer who could produce a book that would move and enlighten, and that in my own 'patchwork' way, I had managed to piece together a respectable career after all."

The pattern of one job leading to yet another continued when Vivien's book promotion brought her to the attention of a speaker's bureau. With the confidence and experience honed at all those bar mitzvahs and community events as well as in the classroom, she took on speaking engagements around the country about the Holocaust. Getting paid to speak about a subject she feels passionately about is one perk. There's another too. "For a busy mom of three, even one night in a Marriott Express in Flint, Michigan, can be a welcome respite," she says with a laugh.

More than fifteen years after she started on this uncharted course, Vivien has fashioned a solution of sorts to the work/don't-work dilemma. Yet the struggle continues. "Even though my 'baby' is a strapping seven-year-old boy in full-day school, I have remained unwilling to leave my children for full-time work," she says. "There have been undeniable trade-offs—economically and career-wise—born of my sporadic work life. But the most priceless gift of my life has been the flexibility to truly revel in my great, funny, kids—to savor my time with them during childhoods that are all too fleeting."

With the book finished, she has more spare time and she recently began a well-paying, part-time job writing grants for a nonprofit organization that works with immigrant Soviet Jews. So where do all those layers of work—sandwiched between family, friends, religion, and community—lead her? She recalled a TV show about the nature of happiness in which social scientists said that 50 percent of happiness is a result of our "hard wiring," ingrained since birth. The other 50 percent is dependent on "flow," a concept that the happiest people are those whose lives have a reasonable balance: a solid marriage, enough money to keep a roof over their heads, and religious and/or communal associations. "What I try for is that flow," says Vivien. "It's a never-ending juggling act, but one that I could never achieve, at least not at this time in my life, if a full-time, fast-track job were added to the mix. But what about the flow? And I still dream about that novel . . . "

⚜ Creating Your Own Job for ⚜ Pleasure and Profit

It is not surprising to us that when women retool, some decide to start businesses of their own. What we heard over and over again was that women were fed up with the rigors of the workplace. Punching clocks, running to meet the train, and working for others were hassles that they no longer wanted. For reasons ranging from "It's too soon to go back" to "I can work in my bathrobe," businesses are emerging in basements, garages, and attics. Today more than half of women-owned businesses are home based.[10]

You never know when or where a great business idea will strike. It could happen while your daughter is protecting the goal at a soccer game, during a friendly conversation at a block party, or at a piano recital. If you are contemplating a start-up business, a pad and pen should be your constant companion.

The number of businesses owned by women represents 38 percent of all businesses in the United States.[11] The numbers are even higher for service or retail businesses, of which a staggering 41 percent are women-owned.[12] We are not shocked that this figure continues to climb. We spoke to many women as we researched this book and learned that they know what they want. When women identify a need for something and have a good idea, they run with it. According to the Department of Labor, this trend will continue because "more and more women have found owning their own business a rewarding experience. Not only have women business owners found financial rewards in business ownership, research has shown that business ownership opened doors to other rewards including self-fulfillment."[13]

The investment in being your own boss is threefold: emotional, financial, and yes, physical. Don't let anyone tell you that it is not hard work—but when it works the rewards can be great. Not all new businesses fly. Many women we met improved their odds by doing their homework and by not being discouraged.

Deborah Williams, the wife of the former NBA player and mother of two young children, started her own business designing and manufacturing women's sportswear, a far cry from practicing clinical psychology. "It was serendipity, " she says. "I didn't intend to go into the fashion industry. But I know where the niches are in terms of apparel for women who lead a sports lifestyle. I felt that few people understand women who have sports as part of their life as well as I do, and I really parlayed that."

Deborah is the first to admit that she doesn't have a fashion background, although she looks like a woman with a natural sense of style. But this 1991 Mrs. USA crown holder fesses up to knowing how to organize people and how to set up infrastructures. She had a trial run at putting together an organization four years earlier when she founded the Players' Wives Association.

Deborah also draws on skills that she used in her prior career. Her research skills were strong and helped her surf the Net for business reports on start-up companies and peruse reprints of *Harvard Business Review* case studies. And then there were her people skills and connections. "I started tapping the resources that I have, the connections that I've made, the relationships that I have, to start building a network of the people I knew who had credibility in their areas. I went after a designer because I really don't know design, but I knew conceptually what I wanted to create. I had to bring in somebody who had experience. I started pulling together, slowly but surely, a good team of people, finding people who understood this industry, who could teach me the business."

Then Deborah signed on a number of athletes and their wives as investors because, more important than investing, they could be helpful marketing the line. She realizes how lucky she is to have friends whose endorsements can translate into sales. "Herb is 2,000 percent supportive," says Deborah. "He's always been involved with the marketing. He's been involved with finding resources for me, finding people who can serve as mentors, and finding marketing opportunities."

This plunge into the garment industry was never in Deborah's game plan. "I would have laughed, just laughed. Timing is everything." Like most start-ups, Her Game 2 is taking more time than expected, but she still went to a good number of home games to cheer Herb on. "Players like looking up in the stands, seeing their wives giving little messages. I think for your relationship to remain healthy, you need to do those things for your husband. Be a part of his life, otherwise it is going to be difficult because you just don't have enough time to cultivate the relationship." After games, they shared a quiet dinner and a long ride home.

Not everyone goes out and rents office space as Deborah did. Because women are looking for business opportunities that have little overhead and are also family friendly, there are an astounding 3.5 million women-owned, home-based businesses.[14] When Cookie Levine of Phoenix wanted a "real" job to help pay family expenses—camp, lessons, educational trips

—she found that there were not many opportunities for forty-six-year-old housewives. Yet it's not as if Cookie hadn't been working all the years her children were growing up. She was a volunteer on community advisory councils, a consumer advocate for a local health agency, and a two-term president of her local Planned Parenthood chapter. "My husband was busy tilting at windmills, righting wrongs, and playing 'Dudley Doright,'" says Cookie. "I realized that I was expending a great deal of energy on 'volunteer' activities and not getting the respect of society because my work couldn't be measured in dollars. I did not have the money to buy a business, but I did have the energy to start a business." A yard sale with a friend raised $4,000 that became the seed money for Levine Linens. "We then took our $4,000 and started buying up antique linens and reselling them to interior design studios. We contacted 'pickers' in England, who would send us merchandise. It very quickly became clear that this might be 'fun,' but it was no money maker. I bought my partner out after ten months, added new linens, contacted architects and designers, and attempted to educate them to include the product in their specifications and budgets. I showed them how to enhance the sale of beds and tables by including products that went on the beds and tables. The next logical step was to add china, crystal, silver, etcetera."

Cookie obtained a "home business occupancy" permit and uses rooms in her house to showcase her samples. Levine Linens now offers more than five thousand different patterns of porcelain. She travels to Europe several times a year to ferret out unique merchandise.

Europe was also a business destination for Lisa Luttrell-Welti, who lived a whirlwind life as a freelance makeup artist in Italy and Paris. Today, as mom of a stepson and two young children, she spends about three days each month in New York City doing makeup for models who appear in commercials. And that's just one aspect of her work world that keeps her connected to her first career. "I felt I always had to have choices. I don't want to feel limited," Lisa says. Because friends and family compliment her home—she adds the artistic touches herself, like faux painting on furniture and walls—she and a friend decided to start a business called Eclectic Expressions. Following a houseware-party format, she will be selling home accessories and personal and gift items. She will offer everything from food to hand-painted furniture.

At the same time, Lisa has received a patent approval for a very hush-hush invention, only saying it is a baby item. How does she have the time to do it all? "My husband has to be on my team," she says. "I could not do any of the things I was doing if he wasn't supportive. I'm really trying not to pass up any opportunity that strengthens me as a person."

———◦———

We know it's not easy to go against the grain and do the unconventional, living a lifestyle that, admittedly, doesn't suit everyone. It's not easy to bathe two babies while your husband is off on a business trip to Berlin. It's not easy to stand in line wearing sweats at the grocery store, eyeing all the carefully coiffed women in business suits. It's not easy to plan day trips for a family vacation while the dual-career family down the block is going to Disney, again!

Sacrifices? Perhaps, depending on how you view the choices. And that's our point. What makes the difference for us and other new traditional wives is looking at life over the long term. What's going to matter to us as wives and mothers in ten or fifteen years? What career possibilities may be there for us even if we jump off the work merry-go-round? What's life without taking some risks? And what is life without choices? As Debbie Ouellet, of Loretto, Ontario, wrote in her letter to the *Toronto Star*, "Liberation is freedom—the freedom to choose. Every woman and every man has the right to choose. So long as you're doing what you want, as long as you can look in the mirror each morning and say, 'That's me and I like it,' you've reached the pinnacle of gender liberation. So, no apologies. I've finally found me. And I like her."[15]

3

Starring in a
Supporting Role

WIFE. Wedding toasts celebrate the new title, but after the honeymoon the word "wife" is often treated like the gift crystal and china: stored away for occasional, but certainly not daily, use. Some cultural commentators have gone one step further and, in efforts to equalize gender roles, have buried the word in a 1950s time capsule. Take a look, for example, at *The New York Times Magazine* special issue on women and the millennium: "From almost every perspective women's lives have been transformed, whether they're mothers or workers, consumers or leaders," notes the introduction.[1] The role of wife received little mention in the introduction or anyplace in the issue.

So where did she go? For centuries—from cave to suburb—the wife's work had been clearly defined: take care of
the husband and children, cook the meals, clean the house, do
the chores. Of course, a wealthy wife was the exception. She
didn't actually perform those tasks; she supervised them.
Regardless of economic status, the wife was expected to be
the caretaker of hearth and home.

ᑫᐤ The Corporate Wife Evolves ᑫᐤ

The twentieth century saw other changes in a wife's role,
beyond the domestic duties. Of course, there have always
been women deeply involved in their husbands' careers:
what's a king without a queen? But it was only after World
War II, when thousands of men marched off to business in
their gray flannel suits and white starched shirts, that the "corporate wife" emerged. Her main task was to free her husband
of all household responsibilities so he could fully concentrate
on his work. Entertaining at home, fund-raising for the right
charities, and attending company functions were also part of
the package. Most of all, she was expected to show the same
unquestioning allegiance to the parent corporation as her
husband did. In many circles it's still an accepted fact of life
that a man cannot succeed in the highest levels of American
business without a wife to serve as his official hostess, hand
holder, and all-around helpmate.

In 1993, when *The Wall Street Journal* surveyed the CEOs
of one hundred leading industrial companies, 95 percent said
that their wives stayed at home with young children.[2] Although conventional wisdom holds that this pattern will

change as younger men in dual-career marriages climb the corporate ladder, studies have found otherwise. It's the thirty-something guy with a wife, kids, and house in the suburbs—just like his fifty-something boss—who is more likely to get a promotion. "There's a whole sociological phenomenon that we are most comfortable around people most like us," says Linda Stroh, a professor of organizational behavior at Loyola University, Chicago. "The captains of industry have wives at home who take care of the children. When looking for a set of managers who are committed and loyal to the organization and who they can trust, they find those traits embedded in someone just like them. It's not a conscious act; it's very much unconscious." Professor Stroh also found that husbands with stay-home wives tended to earn more than husbands in dual-career couples.[3] So it's not surprising that many corporate wives see themselves as part of a team. In a 1998 *Fortune* magazine poll, 57 percent of women replied that the duties of corporate wife—travel, entertaining, charity work, child rearing, and housework—are extremely important to a husband's success.[4]

One corporate wife made headlines in 1998 when she sued her husband for half of his $100 million worth, based on her logical conclusion that she was half responsible for his success. *The Boston Globe* noted, "Gary Wendt has had a stellar twenty-year career at General Electric Company and now, at age fifty-four, is one of its top executives. His wife, Lorna, fifty-three, has been behind him every step of the way—giving advice on job applicants, making small talk with foreign dignitaries, even minding the offspring of colleagues. Now, they are getting divorced, and Mrs. Wendt wants exactly half their assets—a reflection she says of her career as a 'corporate wife.'"[5] Although she did not get the $50 million she wanted, Lorna Wendt was eventually awarded $20 million by a Connecticut judge.

Testifying about the importance of Mrs. Wendt's unpaid contributions to her husband's career was Myra Strober,[6] a Stanford University professor who has studied successful executives. Professor Strober examined the career paths taken by the classes of '81 from Stanford and Tokyo Universities in her recent book, *The Road Winds Uphill All the Way: Gender, Work, and Family in the United States and Japan*. One of her key findings was that wives like Mrs. Wendt are not becoming "historical artifacts," not as long as there are men who pursue the kind of "killer career" it takes to climb to the top of the corporate pyramid. "It's impossible to raise a family with two people both having superstar careers, especially with the husband having a killer career," she says.

But as Professor Strober found in her study, many women are not so eager to back burner their own careers, especially the wives of fledgling captains of industry. "These men are often married to women who are highly educated and high achievers. That's who those men are attracted to." she said.

❧ Two People, One Career ❧

Why would any smart, ambitious woman who could have a fast-track career willingly cut back for the sake of her husband's work? Because the new traditional wife has completely reinvented the role, throwing away the old handbook and rewriting the rules to satisfy her needs as well as her husband's. We spoke with dozens of educated women married to men with demanding careers, both in corporations and in other fields—medicine, law, education, religion, politics, sports, and entertainment. While the reasons varied, the essence was the same: most women believed the demands of dual killer-careers drained them, leaving them without emotional or physical energy for anything else. They simply did not want a breakneck, every-minute-programmed, hired-help-from-kitchen-to-kids lifestyle.

The feminist movement managed to raise the consciousness of even corporate America, so few big companies still expect an executive's wife to play an official role. Yet there are women, in and out of the corporate world, who choose to play a significant role in their husbands' careers. We've dubbed this scenario, "two people, one career."

W. Jay Hughes, an associate professor of sociology at Georgia Southern University, calls the women in this two-for-one arrangement "career wives." She has studied the career wives of missionaries, military officers, and university presidents and found that "many of these women not only 'see a need to play' the role of career wife, but they consider the contributions made by career wives valuable—to society, the organization, their husbands, and themselves—and derive personal satisfaction from 'filling' (v. 'playing') the role of career wife."[7]

That was the case when Anne Moss's husband, Jim, was named publisher of the *Centre Daily Times*, a midsized newspaper that plays an influential role in State College, Pennsylvania, home to Penn State University. The move brought more than a new house and schools in an area affectionately called "Happy Valley" by its residents. It also brought high visibility in community and college activities for both Jim and

Anne, a former print and television model. Happy Valley was a new kind of challenge, but it didn't take long for Anne to adapt to the two-for-one role, from serving on community arts boards to helping with the search for a new arts and architecture dean. "As the wife of the publisher, I felt this was a way I could support Jim in what he was doing," Anne says. "I enjoyed it because it served a purpose for me too. What I was looking for was an opportunity that would help me continue to grow—the arts are something I love—and at the same time would allow me to be supportive of Jim. I think I enhanced who and what he is professionally. A lot of the things that I did to help strengthen the community were rewarding for me personally and professionally. He benefited as well as the paper. So I thought of it as a win-win for everybody."

Anne's public role extended beyond Jim's position because there were few African Americans in State College, the nine-month-a-year home to forty thousand college students. "All of a sudden I was in Happy Valley, in the middle of nowhere, with two kids and a husband, and we were minorities," Anne recalls. "For many of those people, we were the only black experience that they have ever had up close; there was a responsibility level. Maybe we were supposed to open the eyes and broaden the perspective of some people."

Even as part of a two-for-one package, new traditional wives do not play a subservient role in their marriage. They see themselves as equal partners, collaborating on creating a shared life, with a sense of "being in this together." The parallel is a business partnership. In many arrangements, the partners play different roles, drawing on their individual strengths.

The goal is for the whole to equal more than the sum of the parts. The same is true for these wives. They are independent, yet they cherish their interdependence. They practice what library shelves of how-to-improve-your-marriage books preach without even reading them. No one keeps a scorecard: "You got that, so I deserve this." Certainly there are problems, but these couples approach those problems with a spirit of compromise.

The women we met share some similar characteristics, especially empathy, caring, and cooperation. They are seemingly blessed with high levels of EQ, "emotional intelligence," which author Daniel Goleman describes in his best-selling book as awareness of one's feelings, awareness of the feelings of others, managing one's moods, staying motivated and optimistic, and interacting well with other people.[8] "If you want a happy, enduring marriage, your EQ, not your IQ, can make the difference," writes Goleman. "Decades of marital research shows that it is how a couple handles emotional flash points—the hurts and irritations inevitable in an intimate relationship—that determines whether the marriage will last. The most stable unions are among couples who have found ways to air differences without escalating into personal attacks or retreating into stony silence."[9]

What are the other characteristics of a woman who chooses to make her husband's career a priority? Why do some women say "okay," while others say "no way"? Dr. Willa Bernhard,[10] a New York psychologist who has counseled hundreds of women, does not think that these wives have a unique psychological makeup. Rather, she says there is "a constellation of qualities they are more likely to possess":

- They see their role as important and significant.
- They see the power behind the throne as power.
- They enjoy making other people comfortable and happy.
- They are adept at meeting the demands their roles impose.
- They either postpone careers or choose less demanding careers.
- They like the life their husbands' careers afford them.
- They may even love their husbands.

In all fairness, we recognize that not all women—even some who possess one or more of these seven qualities—are comfortable in this kind of relationship. According to Dr. Bernhard, this is not the best decision for every woman. "Because of many culture changes—expectations that girls and boys should be prepared for work outside their homes, many more career opportunities for women that provide financial independence, a social climate that respects working women, later marriages and more divorces—there are many women who want their fulfillment and security through their own careers and aren't willing to put a husband's career before their own.

"And then too, the 'me' generation has produced more people, women included, who resent putting anyone's need before their own. Many of these women find it very difficult to feel they are the tail on anyone else's kite."

We found dozens of women who possess some of those seven qualities, and spent hours discussing the thoughts and feelings that went into their choices. We decided to look at some of those qualities through the prism of their experiences.

An Important and Significant Role

The scene is a testimonial dinner at the glittering Rainbow Room high above midtown Manhattan. Erica Miller watches as her husband, Charlie, wins yet another award for his innovative liver transplant techniques. "He gave the most wonderful speech, including thanking me for my love and support. His secretary told me that when he practiced the speech and came to the part about thanking me, he broke down three times and cried. Three times! He said just the sweetest things, and he was finally able to say it without crying at the Rainbow Room," Erica recalls. After the speech, Charlie's friends and colleagues told Erica that she should have been up at the podium too, saying, "He'd never be there if it wasn't for you. You deserve that award too." Erica smiles and says, "I'll savor those compliments for a long time."

While Erica, forty-six, doesn't brag about her role in her husband's career, she has been credited for his success often enough that she has learned to accept the compliments graciously. "I've lately come to consider supporting Charlie as my career," she says. Charlie heads a transplant surgery center at Mount Sinai Hospital in New York City. He starts operating at 7:30 A.M. and is often not home to suburban New Jersey until after 9:00 P.M. She takes a certain amount of ribbing from friends and relatives because she expects very little from him around the house. He's not the guy who will fix a leaky faucet or regrout the tub. He has missed his three daughters' school plays, friends' weddings, and countless other events because when a liver becomes available for transplant, he must get to the hospital immediately.

After working a fourteen-hour day, literally saving lives, he comes home to a nice dinner and a wife who massages his tired shoulders. But don't look for an ounce of resentment from Erica. It's just not there. "I feel very lucky," says Erica. "He appreciates me. We have a good relationship. He adores me and appreciates what I do running the house, taking care of the kids, and everything else. Last week he had to tell a patient he had become friendly with that he couldn't take the cancer out of his liver and he was going to die. I couldn't do that; I just couldn't handle it. I am much happier preparing dinner and running the house.

"His work is so important. We sort of agreed that's the way our life is going to be; it's our arrangement. Sometimes friends or relatives will tell me that I wait on Charlie too much, but I just laugh it off. That's our relationship. I like to be nurturing. I like being a wife and mother and making a home."

Erica recalls the day when she realized the importance of Charlie's work. It was in Pittsburgh, where Charlie was training to be a liver transplant surgeon. "I was annoyed because on Thanksgiving Day just as we were sitting down to eat he got a phone call that a liver was found," she told us, "and off he went to get it. The next Thanksgiving a huge bouquet arrives in New Jersey with a card: 'Thanks for giving Charlie to me last Thanksgiving so I could have my transplant.' What a jerk I was; I was upset because he wasn't there for turkey. He was saving this woman. She sent bouquets every Thanksgiving for eight years until she died."

Erica wasn't reared to catch a doctor for a husband. Flashback to the early 1960s and an immigrant neighborhood in Newark, New Jersey. Erica is the valedictorian of her eighth-grade class; she stands on the stage and gives her speech but neither parent is there to hear it. Her mother, who has a learning disability and can't read or write, couldn't find her way to the school; her father, a factory worker, was afraid to ask for time off. The graduation was emblematic of her childhood. "My mom was Polish and my father Czech, and both grandparents were immigrant. The extended family had a strong sense of tradition and would get together on holidays such as Christmas Eve for dinner. I just loved being with my family, especially my aunts who quilted and baked bread. My mom was not that way. She was very caring and selfless but just limited. I saw my relatives making loving dinners with a nice sense of style and I wanted to create that." Erica's dream was for a warm, nurturing home life.

Erica's parents did not want her to go to college; they suggested she get married and raise a family. Erica rebelled against that idea and instead paid her own way through The Philadelphia College of Arts, graduating with a weaving degree. She headed to California to live with a girlfriend and before long was weaving tapestries for Tinseltown clients. A blind date hooked her up with a young surgeon in training, Charlie Miller, who pleaded with her to come back East.

Erica readily admits that it has not been an easy path at times. "I am alone a lot because of his hours," she says. "He never goes to a back-to-school night. I was in a store the other day with him and saw a teacher who said, 'Oh, I never met your husband.' A lot of times I go to places where everyone is a couple except me. I wish he were there more. I tell him I feel like a widow sometimes. He says, 'I feel bad but I had a meeting of the board of directors of the transplant center.' I can't get angry but that's the way I feel. The feeling passes and I don't hold it against him; if we have a problem he is there." She doesn't rail against the inevitable. If Charlie can't be there, he can't, so she picks and chooses her social situations. She attends school events but politely declines wedding invitations. Why set herself up to feel left out when everyone else is dancing?

Yet every time Erica has needed to lean on Charlie, he has come through for her. When her father died suddenly, Charlie left work in the middle of the day to come home, comfort her, and take over all the arrangements, to be the "fixer" at home that Erica usually is. "He was very supportive and really wonderful. Everything I normally do, he did. In a situation like that, he was there. He was off from being a surgeon."

Erica and Charlie's marriage is a win-win partnership. Charlie, obviously a gifted surgeon, pursues his passion; his wife reaps deep satisfaction in knowing that she's helping her husband save lives.

We found several wives who share a special sense of connection to their husband's career because they once worked in the same field. That's the case for Maureen and David Canary. David is known to millions as the good twin/bad twin in the TV soap opera, *All My Children*. Maureen, fifty-one, a petite, perky redhead, is an actor as well. Her professional career began at age eighteen, but Maureen says that she wanted to be in show business since she was four years old. After more than a decade of singing and dancing on stages from Broadway to Boulder, she has opted for a quieter life with David, two children, and a dog in a gentrified community where she spends more time in carpools than at casting calls. Married since 1982, the Canarys seem like a typical suburban couple. David dashes to catch a commuter train to his job in New York City; Maureen remains in the 'burbs of

Connecticut, juggling parent-teacher conferences, religious school, karate, and dance lessons. While her role is behind the scenes, it's an essential part in making their marriage a success.

"I think you have to know what your role is and accept it," says Maureen, looking more like a diva than a den mother in her leopard-print pumps and velour pants ensemble. "You have to find a real sense of serenity with the choice that you have made. And as David said to me so eloquently yesterday, 'You know, this really was a choice. You didn't drop out of show business.' And I didn't. I felt that children were very, very important to me. Also, I have no sense of frustration about 'I could've done this, I could've done that.'

"I was thinking about David and why the best option is to put our combined energies into his career. A lot of women say they can do both. I think you can do both, but I don't think that *I* could do both and do even one of them well. I think I would do a disservice to both of them. I would not be as good an actress as I was when I was 100 percent committed to playing a role, and I would be not as good a mother. Yes, you can have it all, you just can't have it all at the same time. This is all about priority."

In a New England town further up the seaboard, another wife shares the same sensibility. Most houses in Provincetown, the artsy tourist hamlet at the tip of Cape Cod, are covered by weathered gray shingles. One house stands out with its white columns and a brick facade covered in ivy and wisteria. Since 1984, this former convent has been the summer home of Norman Mailer, the two-time Pulitzer Prize winner, and Norris, his wife of almost twenty years.

This home is clearly her design, with a dramatic curved sofa and luminous avocado green walls filled with her paintings. The most recent, a splash of brilliant color over the fireplace, captures Norris, Norman, and a friend sharing drinks at a Havana bar. Norris painted the realistic portraits, which *People* magazine pronounced "bizarre but compelling." Family photographs are at every turn; fifty-one cover one tabletop alone. A painting of Norman hangs, icon like, in a gilded frame. Nine his-hers-ours children, aged twenty-one to fifty and scattered across North and South America, visit for weeks at a time each summer. To Norris they are all "our" children, as much a part of her life as Norman's.

It's clear to a casual observer that not only has she decorated the set but that Barbara Davis Norris Church Mailer is also the producer and director of this family saga. As she explains in her soft drawl, "Norman writes and I do everything else."

When Norris married Norman she assumed monumental responsibilities, namely giving her husband the freedom to concentrate on writing his epic books. Norris's critical role as wife and mother became clear shortly after their 1980 wedding when she realized that the cost of alimony to several wives, children in private schools, his secretary, and other expenses had left Norman's finances in disarray. Her common sense told her what needed to be done and she did it; she did not play prima donna, demanding this famous writer provide her with a staff for the household and business. If Norman needed someone to run his house and finances, to provide a comfortable nest for the children who came in and out of their life, to lend a sympathetic ear, then Norris would do that. She put aside her successful modeling and fledgling acting career, passing up runway work in Europe and tryouts in L.A.

This hands-on approach might not be typical of a Manhattan literary socialite, yet Norris is anything but typical. She spent most of her life in Arkansas until Norman, passing through on a book tour in 1975, convinced her to come to New York to try modeling. "You can't hire someone to run your life. You've got to take care of it yourself," she says with a no-nonsense attitude that is probably genetically linked to her sharecropper grandparents. "One thing I have learned over the years is that you can't have a career that takes up all your time and still be a good mother. Something suffers and usually it's the kids. I didn't want my kids to suffer."

Marrying a famous man, and then assuming full responsibility for his life, has worked because he has made her a partner in his success. He asks her to read his works-in-progress, give her opinion of business deals, collaborate on screenplays, and accompany him on book tours. "I have handled it pretty well because of him," Norris says. "He always makes me feel important, like I am his equal. He lets me read the manuscripts and do my little edit, and we talk about the work he's doing. I feel very much a part of it."

While Loretta's husband wasn't saving lives, starring in soap operas or writing prize-winning novels like the husbands of Erica, Maureen, and Norris, he was building a career in corporate America. "To this day Vic says, 'I could not have done it without you' and that makes me feel pretty great," Loretta says. "When I dig deep within myself, I realize that what is so special about him saying that—besides the fact that it is a lovely compliment—is that when we were college kids together I always believed that I could do whatever he did and that someday I would. But it didn't take long for me to realize that there could not be two Vics in our house. He needed to know that I was there for the children and the plumber and that I could make a quick turn around into an evening gown for a movie premiere on either coast. I knew that what I did for him was important and that he was proud of me. But what really kept me going was that I also knew without a doubt that when my time came, he would be as supportive."

❧ The Power behind the Throne ❧

When we went to Maureen's stunning, sun-filled home in southern Connecticut, we spotted a statue wedged between the cookbooks on a shelf in the kitchen. At first glance it looks like a bookend, but it doesn't take more than a moment to realize that the shiny figurine is, in fact, an Emmy. When Maureen's husband, David Canary, received that Emmy in 1994 for Outstanding Lead Actor for his portrayal of Adam and Stuart Chandler in *All My Children*, he dedicated it to her on a program seen by millions of viewers worldwide.

Maureen recalls his words: "I'm married to this wonderful actress in her own right who put her career on hold to raise our beautiful children," he said. "She saved my life and she is my life. This is for you, Maureen." As he finished his moving acceptance speech, cameras panned from David to Maureen. "I wish I could have been more composed at that moment, but I never expected him to say that. I was crying. It was great. That's what keeps our relationship working. He made that a moment for both of us," she says.

When David is nominated for an Emmy, he relies on Maureen to screen hundreds of tapes with him before deciding which shows to submit to the judges. "I consider myself probably a good deal more of a partner to David than a lot of women do because we were in the same business. We were both actors when we met. We understand each other's jargon when we speak. And if he needs help with a scene, he knows he can get it from me because he does respect my ability. Because as I said, I didn't flunk out of show business, I made a conscious choice. He picks my brain; he utilizes my professional expertise to a great extent, because it is often very difficult for him to be totally objective about what he is doing. He says, 'Turn the TV on and watch the scene that I did with Marcy the other day.'"

Almost twenty years ago Maureen urged David to try out for a TV soap. When David landed the part on *Search for Tomorrow* he found, as Maureen had predicted, that it was fast-paced, challenging work. Then "all my kiddies," as Maureen calls it, came along in 1983. Their son, Chris, was born on November 26 and David started work on December 6, and he's been on ever since. "What a great gig," Maureen says. "I knew I didn't have to work. And I knew I could do things periodically, but there was no way that I was going to leave this baby in the first year of his life."

For Maureen, it seems as if she had been rehearsing for this supportive role—not to be confused with subordinate—much of her professional life. "I'm much happier singing duet than solo on stage. I'm more relaxed," she tells us. "A part of me really wants to be on the sideline and not be the center of attention."

Before speaking to us, Maureen wrote about her choices, allowing feelings from deep within her to surface. There were thoughts she had never before put into words; thoughts came so fast and furious that her hand hurt from writing. "It might have been nice to be a star. I don't know. But I can tell you that the women David works with—some of them very, very big stars—often say to him how they envy him and my staying home with the kids. It's not a sexist thing, because I think women should do what they feel they need to do. Some of them would not be happy at home with kids. They need to work."

David doesn't hesitate to praise and thank Maureen, not only in private but in public too. That admiration from David reaffirms her choices. She interprets her husband's praise as his way of thanking her for her commitment to the family and making her feel that she is still part of the business. "This is my wife," he often says when introducing her. "She's the real talent." Words like that make Maureen feel pretty special, and it doesn't take long to realize that she is a grounded woman with a solid, positive sense of self. She feels secure about her partnership with her husband, about the choices that she made, and about her talent.

Sharon Beeler qualifies as another "power behind the throne." The wife of cowboy artist Joe Beeler, she has partnered and promoted his career as both a painter and sculptor. "I just had a date with a genius," Sharon McPherson told her mom after she returned from her first date with the young artist in June 1956. Six weeks later they were engaged and a few months later married.

It took years for the public to recognize what Sharon knew from day one. The Beelers struggled financially while he tried to sell his western paintings of cowboys and Native Americans. But Sharon never lost faith, always believing that Joe's artistic talents were destined to be applauded. Living with a new baby in a rented cabin on Five Mile Creek in northeastern Oklahoma, Sharon learned how to whip up suppers from the squirrels and rabbits that Joe hunted. In 1961, realizing that a more lucrative market existed in the West, Sharon, Joe, their baby daughter, Tracy, and an overloaded U-Haul headed to red-rock country. They settled in Sedona, Arizona, were their son, Jody, was born. Sharon believed that this small northern Arizona community near the majestic Oak Creek Canyon would provide inspiration for her husband. It was here that Sharon began managing the business side of Joe's career, while he retreated to his studio to paint and sculpt.

Sharon ushered packs of prospective buyers, many vacationing in nearby Phoenix, through their house, which doubled as an art gallery for Joe's paintings and sculptures. Some people called ahead; others gave her little warning. "They'd come by and look at the art," she says. "We'd have to have the house immaculate in five minutes. The kids would just throw things in the closet and look marvelous and wonderful. At times I was very happy doing what I was doing, and there were times that I wasn't exactly thrilled about forty-five people coming in the house. But it was worth it and fun, and Joe and I didn't disagree on anything."

Even in hindsight Sharon, who had majored in art and business in college and planned a career in advertising, admits no regrets about putting her own ambitions aside. "Oh, I think there was a time that I did sacrifice; I didn't know it," she says, laughing. "It was a wonderful thing that we were doing and we were busy working toward the same goal, so I didn't feel I was sacrificing anything."

Thirty-eight years after dragging that U-Haul hundreds of miles, Sharon is still supporting Joe's career. She no longer has to push his art—Joe is recognized as one of the preeminent western artists in America—but she continues to be part of the Beeler family business. "It's fallen to me to do all the bookkeeping. It started out with a little simple checkbook and just went on into investing," Sharon explains, adding in a matter-of-fact tone, "somebody had to do it."

Not far from the studio where Joe paints, Sharon has her own studio in a barn. She is quick to explain that her paintings are very different from Joe's art. "I do this off-the-wall modern stuff, and he really thinks that it's strange," says Sharon. Although she has sold some of her pieces, she has never thought about it as a business. "I just couldn't do it all. You know, my priorities. My first thing wasn't that. Joe's career is what we're into and it takes both of us."

⌒ They Enjoy Making Other ⌒ People Comfortable and Happy

When we thought about "making other people comfortable and happy," we realized that happiness wears many faces. There are creature comforts like hot chocolate after shoveling snow on a freezing morning or a fluffy towel after a warm shower, and there are cerebral comforts like knowing that the children are home, safely tucked in bed, or gathering your family around the dinner table and sharing the day's activities. Before we spoke to other women, we sat down and had a heart-to-heart talk about why we get so much psychic satisfaction making our own families feel comfortable and nurtured. Indeed that had been one of the initial attractions of our friendship. We each realized that we had found a simpatico soul who was not embarrassed to talk about the pleasure derived from doing little things (and big) for our families. And it *is* pleasure, not guilt or some warped sense of duty.

Even when we were buried under this manuscript, Loretta managed to oversee a major home renovation; Mary planned a mini-vacation for the family and packed her oldest son off to college. It would have been easy, and justifiable, to put these tasks aside under the pressure of a book deadline. We didn't because making our families happy makes us happy. However, we also agreed in our little chat that we don't want our efforts taken for granted or to go unrecognized. An approving smile, a high-five from our husband or children, or a hug and a kiss is our adult equivalent of a gold star. We suspect that other wives feel the same way.

From Christmas dinner for thirty to having a revolving door for family and friends in their Provincetown home, Norris Mailer brings her southern hospitality and affability to everything she does. Watching her in action for a few hours one summer morning, we quickly understood how Norris makes not only Norman, but the entire entourage, comfortable and happy. While Norman toiled on the third floor on yet another project, Norris managed the flow on the main floor. Her son from her first marriage, Matthew, came in with his German girlfriend, both sweating from tennis. They are fledgling film directors trying to raise a half-million dollars to produce their screenplays. Norris beamed, rattling off the awards that Matthew had won, her arm around his shoulder. She chatted briefly with her son-in-law who was watching his daughter and her friend frolic in the bay with two dogs. She answered a phone call from her then eighteen-year-old son, John, her only biological child with Norman, who asked her to bring his P-town Pizza logo shirt to the restaurant where he worked. No problem. We all headed out to bring him his "uniform," passing up trendy Provincetown restaurants for lunch at a waterside pizza parlor. As we sat there, it seemed like Norris enjoyed getting a glimpse of John at work. We both can understand the way she felt.

Like thousands of other American women, Erica Miller admires the Martha Stewart way of doing things. In fact, some might even say she looks like Martha, tall with straight blonde hair, dressing casually in sweaters and pants. Although she is not about to decoupage brown grocery bags to make wrapping paper, she loves to weave, paint, sew, and spin yarn. Laughing, she admits that her friends tease her because she folds napkins intricately even for weekday dinners.

Erica delights in making a beautiful home for Charlie and their three daughters, taking pleasure in the details. Her home is a showcase for her artistic talents from the tapestries on the wall to her carefully coordinated interior design. "There are a lot of small things important to your own well being," she says. "I buy some flowers at the grocery store and put them in a bowl on the kitchen table. I get enjoyment every time I walk by. I stop and look. It's so nice, the way the petals are opening and the sun is shining on them."

Making others comfortable also means taking care of mundane matters. Maureen Canary doesn't hesitate to rattle off the downside. "Yes, I do get annoyed sometimes. I do feel that many of the jobs that I tend to could be done by someone with no job qualifications whatsoever. Cleaning toilets, ironing, and folding laundry; it doesn't require any great gifts. So I do feel sometimes that I'm highly over-qualified to be doing what I do in my life, but you accept that as a whole package. When I was a full-time actress in New York, I still had to do the laundry and clean the toilet."

☙ Adept at Meeting the Demands ❧ Their Role Imposes

It's one thing to help your husband chase his dream if he's practicing his profession in your hometown, tinkering with some honey-I-shrunk-the-kids invention in the attic, or burning the midnight oil working an international deal at corporate headquarters. But what if his dream means leaving life as you know it, moving to a strange city where the new boss has warned "rent, don't buy," and your husband's actions will be scrutinized by a hostile media?

Obviously that calls for an extraordinary level of support and a leap of faith. It also puts us in a double bind when our husbands look to us for advice: should he go for it or is the scenario just too risky? Can he succeed in the job? Can we manage all the stress on the family and adjust to a new life? If we give the green light and it works out, everyone's happy. If the venture fails, then the marital fallout can be disastrous. We not only have to soothe his bruised ego, but we must also make sure our own feelings don't turn hostile. How do we do that? Add to that the fact that when we actively support our husband's career, without a doubt we are more invested in both his successes and failures. As partners, the ups and downs hit us harder.

Ali Torre, forty, wife of New York Yankees manager Joe Torre, will never forget how she felt the night her husband's team clinched the 1996 World Series. "It was so intense. I really couldn't believe it. It's really hard to describe how I felt, except I was so happy—a dream come true. I started screaming and then I took off running through the stadium. I saw a security guard and he said, 'Go ahead.' I saw Joe standing up on this platform all by himself. Our eyes met and I ran up and he hugged me. It was really a big moment." She continues, "Joe's dream became my dream. It's something we thought about and dreamed about. That was his goal. I told him that once he got to the World Series I was retiring from baseball. I've been very supportive and into it. We've been together for fifteen years. I love watching him manage. It becomes an addiction for me because it is so much a part of our life."

That's the happy ending. But there were no guarantees that that would be the case when Joe accepted the offer to manage the Yankees. Both Torres are realists and not new to the game. They knew the stats: Joe's playing career, which spanned the years from 1960 to 1977, was short of a World Series win. Then came his three manager positions—the Braves, Cardinals, and Mets—all ending with pink slips. (Ali vividly remembers his less-than-gracious dismissal from the Mets, which occurred only two weeks after she met Joe.) They both knew that only two of Joe's sixteen predecessors survived a second season under Yankee's owner George Steinbrenner.

We first met Ali at her rented home overlooking the Long Island Sound. The entrance foyer was strewn with packing cartons. It would be their fifth move in ten years. The first World Series win meant they could buy a house without worrying whether Joe would get fired. "George told us 'Rent, don't buy,'" Ali says, referring to Steinbrenner's less-than-subtle suggestion when Joe first arrived for the job.

For those of us who refuse to let go of old stereotypes, being a supportive wife might imply an inequality in the relationship. In fact, many of the women we met, like Ali, were emphatic about the equality in their marriages. These women are brave enough to buck the cultural trend, making choices that work best for them, their husbands, and their families. Silent partners? Not really. In many cases these vocal women are sounding boards for their husbands. Important issues are bandied around the bedroom. Should I take on this new client? Are my prices too high? How should I react to this problem? What about this hard decision?

Connie Sargent, forty-two, and her husband, John, met at business school. Connie worked for ten years, first as a product manager for General Foods and then in an advertising agency where she ran the CBS account. John went into publishing and is now the president of Holtzbrink Publishing, owners of St. Martin's Press among other book houses. Connie is not involved in his day-to-day work but says that she is John's sounding board. It was not so long ago that John had to make a major business decision: should he or shouldn't he publish Peter Morton's book about Monica Lewinsky? Connie remembers that day vividly because John telephoned her several times. "It was so exciting and at the time it was very questionable," she says. "It was before the impeachment proceedings and after the elections, and no one knew if the thing was going to go away. He called and said, 'Okay, what do you think? What do you think about this much money? Do you think it would sell that many copies?' Honestly, I don't know the answers to those questions; I'm not in this business. For him I was a sounding board, somebody to just talk to about it."

Postponing a Career or Choosing a Less Demanding One

Despite the reality that most women can't do it all and have it all, the media still promotes the fantasy of a woman who effortlessly puts in a fifty-hour week at the office and bakes cookies for the Brownie troop she leads. That old perfume commercial "I can bring home the bacon, fry it up in the pan and never never let you forget you're a man" keeps playing in our subconscious, and any less than doing-it-all is failure. Women who dare reject the male model of success are often regarded as traitors to the cause. Yet many of us harbor a not-so-secret desire for another, better kind of life. Survey after survey has found that many parents, particularly well-educated professionals, work longer hours than ever, and many wish they could slash their time on the job. Federal studies show that couples overall were employed ten hours more a week in 1997 than in 1970.[11] For those of us who pursued college and beyond the payoff may be higher salaries . . . and longer work weeks. A survey of sixty thousand Americans found that one out of three male managers works fifty hours a week or more as compared with one in five men in less demanding jobs. For women, it's one in six vs. one in fourteen.[12]

Let's face it. Despite flextime, paternity leave, and an array of other programs to make it easier to parent, it's not considered macho for most men to announce at the office that they'll be leaving early every Thursday to go grocery shopping. Many do it . . . furtively or on weekends. Maybe it's okay to coach a son's Little League team or a daughter's soccer team. That's cool and something to joke or brag about—depending on the team's success—at lunch. Too often even those duties end up in the wife's lap. A friend whose husband volunteered to coach a soccer team suddenly found herself in charge when he had to go on several sudden business trips. She was just starting a new, part-time job as a real estate agent. There she was, racing to show a house, then home to find the cleats and soccer ball, then up to the soccer field to coach a team of second-grade girls. "I had them running in circles. What do I know about soccer?" she says plaintively.

Most wives don't earn as much as their husbands; women still make seventy-three cents for every dollar men earn.[13] When the big decision is made that the two-career life isn't working and one is going to cut back, it's not surprising that it's the wife who gets the going-away luncheon. Some cultural critics will argue that wives have been duped into thinking that they—not their husbands—must stay home. The women we found are not brainwashed. They are smart, thoughtful, and articulate, and there are millions more like them across the country. What's fascinating is that most repeated the same two reasons for cutting back: first, they wanted to stay home more than their husbands did. They wanted to be the nurturers, to find some balance, to bring some peace and harmony to their lives. Second, they were ready for a change from the work world. Most had worked since their teenage years: been there, done that. They were ready for a new adventure and if it was tending the home fires instead of slaying dragons, well, that suited them just fine. Yet for most of the women we talked to, that new adventure at home eventually included something they didn't expect: work. Maybe paid, maybe not, but some kind of work— when they were ready, on terms they wanted—that would use their skills and talents.

When her daughters entered their teenage years and needed less direct supervision, Erica, the surgeon's wife, realized that she was ready to expand her world. The cultural pressure to "get a real job" was beginning to mount. "I wondered 'Where is my self-worth?'" she recalls. "One part of me felt it was important to stay home and the other part of me wondered whether I should do something else: make a mark in the world." That's part of what sparked her to start the Transplant Liver Center (TLC), a temporary home for transplant patients and their families. "It seemed to make sense, because I was still not going off and doing something completely separate like weaving or running an art gallery. This was doing something supportive of my husband's career. This was okay, not self-indulgent. For what I would get paid, it's not worth my time. My time is better spent helping him to be better with what he does."

Erica had learned that transplant patients' families, with no money for expensive Manhattan hotels, were sleeping during the day on benches in Central Park. She was so disturbed that, working with another physician's wife, she moved ahead at fast-forward speed to create a decent, homey place to stay. Although neither had ever taken on such a venture, they jumped right in, visiting facilities in Pittsburgh and at the Mayo Clinic. They found apartment space in Manhattan near Mount Sinai Hospital and negotiated a deal for three apartments, eventually adding adjoining units. The result was the Transplant Liver Center with ten bedrooms.

The goal was to make people as comfortable as possible. "We wanted it to be like a home away from home. They have their own bedroom, but they share the kitchen and the living room and the dining room, and some bathrooms—sometimes two rooms share a bathroom. We ask forty-five dollars a night, and if they can't pay it, we say, 'How's thirty or how's twenty sound?' We have a cabinet in the back with food—pasta and soups and cereals," Erica says. The families pay on a sliding scale, and Erica organizes a fund-raiser, the Chrysanthemum Ball, every fall. The monthly rent is $10,000 and Erica and her partner pull together the money and they have never missed a payment. Some part-time job!

Like Erica, other women have found their own balance between family and other aspects of life, which sometimes includes work. When somebody at a cocktail party asks Connie Sargent, the publisher's wife, "What do you do?" she told us that her usual answer is, "I'm a mom. I'm at home with my kids." She continues, "At first I thought, hmm, that's not a very exciting thing to say. Over the years what I've found out is that people want to talk about what's happening with kids and their families. They don't think less of you."

Yes, Connie stays home to care for the two children. But she doesn't stay home to watch soaps and eat chocolates or work on her tennis game. She still reads the business section of the newspaper, and she has joined with a group of seven "awesome" mothers (six have master's degrees or more) who gather every Monday morning in a Brooklyn apartment to chat about kids . . . and books. These are serious readers; their reading list includes Salman Rushdie's *Midnight's Children*. The women in her group also volunteer at a job-training center for homeless adults. Connie explains, "I think for me, having kids and taking a break allowed me to redefine myself and create a new identity that has nothing to do with what my job is."

Now that her children are a little older, the same flexibility that prevails in her personal life extends to a new, abbreviated work life. She has fashioned a part-time job doing marketing for a graphic designer for a few hours each week. For Connie, that's enough for right now. The key is balance and remembering what her priorities are. She's comfortable with that amount of time and responsibility on top of her other roles as wife and mother. "That's why it's working so well in our particular marriage, because I don't feel trapped at all, and to have this break here. Now I'm doing something I really love," she says. "I figure I've got twenty-five years ahead of me to go back to work and do something else."

There is no question about it, Ali Torre's career is on hold, and she too is putting her husband's career first. "It's nice to feel that you want to do something for someone," Joe Torre writes in his book, *Chasing the Dream*.[14] "The truth is, Ali already has done so much for me. She's made me into a better, happier person—and a much less guarded one. Ali has been unbelievably supportive. When spring training began, she told me, 'You're going to win the World Series this year. This is the year.'"

While these have definitely been Joe's years, when Ali met Joe, she was concentrating on her own goals, unwilling to put them aside. "My life was in transition. It was a very emotional time for me. My only focus was to graduate from college. My primary goal was to get my bachelor's degree. I did that; I accomplished that," she says proudly.

So it should not come as any big surprise to Joe if Ali decides to follow a dream of her own in the years to come. "I actually wanted him to retire after he won the first World Series. I asked him, 'How long do you plan to continue managing? You reached your goal.' But then I knew that he had to defend his title, and it was something he really wanted to do."

While Ali is not sure what she will do in the future, she is certain that Joe will be there for her in the same way she has been there for him. "I've actually considered going back to get a master's degree in social work because it seems like I'm always going in that direction. I figure that when Joe retires from managing and goes into broadcasting, and Andrea gets a little older, he'll be able to help."

Maureen Canary, too, has a vision of work in the future, and like Ali, it is not quite focused yet. "Everything just sort of conspired to make it possible for me to really do what I wanted to do," she says. "If I had to work, I'd work, but I don't and I have a passion for my children that is like nothing I've ever done before. And I don't feel like I've given up my career. I change with it, and I'll change again."

Maureen may not be singing and strutting on Broadway these days, but she seizes every opportunity to use her God-given talents. Often it's nothing more than an informal song fest with friends and family around the baby grand, but David is always there looking on with admiration and respect. "Somebody starts playing something from *The Secret Garden* and I get up and sing it," she says. "I will see David looking at me and I see that pride."

Recently Maureen and David costarred in a benefit performance of A. R. Gurney's play, *Love Letters*. Maureen says, "Crew members came to me and said, 'You have good comic sense; you have real talent.'" Other admirers asked her, "Where has he been hiding you?"

Who wouldn't feel great hearing these accolades? Yet Maureen doesn't walk around with a swelled head. According to Mo, as her friends call her, the praise is simply an ego booster. Nothing more; nothing less. Maureen is content and comfortable with this arrangement—for now. She doesn't regret putting her theatrical career on hold. But she doesn't see her role as it is today as an "unlimited run" either. She knows that someday she will be back on the stage. "I feel it is important to keep your receptors open and to know who you are as an artist. I'm sure I will go back to work because I need to be fulfilled artistically as well. As Yogi Berra said, 'It ain't over 'til it's over.'"

⌒ They Like the Life Their ⌒ Husband's Career Affords Them

Marlene Wynne of Los Angeles is the caretaker for her clan, a role that she obviously enjoys, takes pride in, and does well. Married for more than thirty years to Bob, a successful attorney turned movie executive turned entrepreneur, Marlene is both a good listener and someone you want to listen to; she exudes a glass-half-full optimism. Somehow she puts a positive spin on situations that others might complain about. This is how she explains life with a husband whose work often demands twelve-hour days: "Most people who are really successful don't work from nine to five. They travel, they have meetings, they have high-pressure positions," she says. "When I was a kid my father had a retail clothing store. He worked three or four nights a week. I came into a married life where I had the same thing. People who aren't in the situation might not understand. They see a man away from home, leaving a woman with three children. 'Goodness,' somebody said to me many years ago, 'how do you stand it that your husband is away all the time?' I never forgot my answer. I said,

'Well, I like my life.'"

Although Marlene worked part-time in a variety of jobs from a women's sportswear showroom rep, to teachers' support staffer, to ESL instructor, she eventually stopped as her home life became more complicated. While she admits that "It would be wonderful to have a fabulous profession," the reality is, "then I'd have to hire a business manager, but I could never turn over my tasks to someone else." Bob urges her to do more, to consider a career, now that the children are grown. Marlene says with a laugh, "I told him, 'Dear, I'm too busy. I don't have time. I'm too busy with our life. Somebody has to be in charge.'"

In charge she is. For two years, wearing a hard hat, she worked full-time with a construction team that built their new home above the beach in Malibu. Marlene, always interested in interior design and construction, had taken courses at a local community college before planning her new house. While she wanted to be well-informed, she did not want to be in charge of the massive project, so she hired a facilitator to work with the contractor and to get all the necessary permits and plan approvals. He never showed up. Marlene clearly loves recounting what happened then: "'This project is not going to get off the ground,' I said to Bob. 'What are we going to do?' He says, 'You're hired.' I said, 'I don't know what to do.' He said, 'You'll figure it out.'" Marlene, a supreme organizer, did just that with the help of the contractor and architect.

She was so flush with success that she helped redo her mother-in-law's home after she and Bob convinced her to move nearby. Doors were moved, drywalls installed, and the whole place redecorated, on a tight budget no less. Marlene even drew up architectural designs. "I learned how to do drafting, so I drafted a small area. I knew about that much," she says making a gesture with her thumb and index finger indicating how little it really was. "I pretended I knew. I pretend really well."

Now that her grown sons live in close proximity, she is truly content. Her family has always been the most important part of her life and having them close is a gift that she doesn't take for granted. Their home, which echoes the splashing sound of Pacific waves, is like a cocoon where the family gathers for Sunday barbecues, birthdays, and holiday celebrations.

Whether we have grown children or toddlers, part of our mothering instinct is to teach them little lessons about life, our own personal parables. So Marlene wants her children to understand that she and Bob worked hard for this life, very hard and hand in hand. "You didn't really know me when I was your age. I had a lot of responsibility—three children already," she explained to one of her adult sons. "It's different; you only see me now. You didn't see me then." To illustrate her point she showed some old home movies with shots of the family at the public parks and beaches. "Why do you think we went there?" she asked. Not waiting for an answer, she quickly said, "Because it was free."

As with Marlene, every woman we talked to emphasized that she feels blessed to have choices about how to live her life.

Sharon Beeler doesn't doubt that she made the right decision to stand her ground next to her artist husband in a storm of cultural change. "We start out with one bunch of values and the values are still there, but the whole world is changing. Things are galloping away, so you really have to hang on." And hang on she did. "There was a time when we were just looked on as peasants," she says. Her friends told her, "You stay home with your husband? Nobody does that. We are going back to school, and we're going to make something of our lives.'"

Sharon never went back to school because not only did she enjoy managing Joe's business, she loved being a mother. "All the kids came to our house because all their mothers were working. I had all the fun with the kids after school because that is when they come home and tell everything. It really wasn't much of a sacrifice because it was so rewarding." She adamantly believes that that decision also had a positive impact on her marriage. "I have a lot of friends who went back to school and are teachers and got jobs and careers," says Sharon. "Most of them are divorced."

⁓ They May Even Love ⁓ Their Husbands

This might seem like a non sequitur. Don't all wives love their husbands? Apparently not, with a 50 percent divorce rate in this country. Among the women we spoke with, the love and affection they all had for their husbands was obvious. They seemed to share some special, unique bond with their soul mates. Maureen tells of her partnership with David and how, in spite of over-scheduled lives, they manage to find the time to keep the sparks alive. "He's very romantic, and he's very dear. He's funny," she says with a smile. "That is the glue. I think the structure of marriage and family is love, loyalty, and honesty. But the laughter is the glue that holds it together. We laugh about everything, we just do."

Sharon shares two key qualities with other women who made the choice to be a new traditional wife. One is that her husband is her best friend, and she believes that makes all the difference in the world. "You have to be best friends and then you can work anything out," she says. The other trait is that she truly believes in the genius of her husband and for her, love means putting aside her own career and joining in his, for a shared life adventure. Of course, not many wives call their husbands "geniuses," but they do believe their husbands have exceptional talents or callings. For these women the decision is simple: If your husband is your lover and best friend why wouldn't you put his career first—for a few years, for a decade, or for a lifetime—especially when you know that he'll do the same for you in return?

ᓚ Supporting...in Other Ways ᓗ

While many wives do not lend such hands-on support to their husbands' work, other women opt for "two-people, one-career." The wife is the family CEO, freeing her husband to pursue a demanding career. For many of us that decision is tied to another choice—motherhood. Choosing motherhood is almost easy compared to all the other decisions: when to become pregnant, how to care for baby, how many children you want. The new traditional wife is stepping into a cultural minefield.

4

Choosing Children over Careers

The scene is the same from Plymouth to Portland, from Chicago to Chattanooga:

Doors are locked, children are in bed, and Mom is just about ready to run in. But not so fast. First, it's into the kitchen to make sandwiches for the next day, set the table for breakfast and put water in Fido's dish. Then as she passes through the living room she notices that the remote is nowhere to be seen. Scouring the furniture, she spies the clicker ready to disappear between the couch cushions and puts it on top of the TV, preventing a family world war in the morning. Spotting one sneaker at the foot of the steps, she searches on hands and knees for its mate, which somehow found its way under a bookcase some twenty yards away.

On her way up the stairs she grabs a crumpled shirt hanging from the banister and then tosses it into the bathroom hamper. Tiptoeing into her bedroom—Dad said "goodnight" some thirty minutes earlier—she spends a minute taking out her clothes for the next morning. As she is about to go into the bathroom for her two minute beauty regimen, she remembers that her youngest needs money for the school book sale. Instead of fumbling in the dark for her purse and wallet, she takes a post-it from the top of her nightstand, writes a large dollar sign and sticks it on the bathroom mirror.

This vignette applauds the multitasking energy of mothers who take care of their families with a sense of love and joy, not resentment. No moaning and groaning, no male bashing, no woe-is-me. In fact, it's just the opposite. It's unclear whether the mother is laying out jeans or a pinstriped suit for the next day; that's deliberate. Maybe she works, maybe she doesn't. The message neatly avoids that cultural minefield.

While some family CEOs work full-time, many we found don't because they are striving to achieve more balance in their lives, a seemingly impossible task with a forty-plus-hours-a-week job, husband, and children. The ideological struggle between those women who chose to stay at home and those who chose to work full-time has been dubbed the "mommy wars," with the battle fought, for the most part, in the media. Not a season goes by without a cannon shot from one side or the other. Globe-trotting *Washington Post* reporter Iris Krasnow wrote of her decision to stay home in *Surrendering to Motherhood: Losing Your Mind, Finding Your Soul.*[1] Volleying back, *New York Times* writer Susan Chira made her case for a demanding career in *A Mother's Place: Taking the*

Debate about Working Mothers beyond Guilt and Blame.[2] Those titles neatly sum up the divide: On one side mothers claim that staying home is not all fun and games, but ultimately it's the most rewarding career a woman can have. The other side argues that a happy mother is a good mother, so a woman should work full-time if she wishes and not worry about the effect on her children. The debate leaves many a woman feeling damned if she does and damned if she doesn't. A New York University sociologist, Kathleen Gerson, who has studied the changing work habits of both men and women, told us that women are facing cultural changes that put them in a bind. "Whatever choice they make is questioned," she says. "If you make the choice not to work, or if you work full-time and try to balance work with child rearing—all those choices have costs and tend to be frowned upon by someone. Women who don't work are accused of being lazy and not carrying their share of the load. Women who do work are accused of neglecting their children."[3]

There even seems to be a discrepancy between what women do and what women think. The statistic often touted in newspaper and magazine articles is that about 70 percent of women work.[4] Public opinion surveys often find strong support for mothers at home. What this statistic doesn't tell is that a considerable number of these women work part-time or from their home. In a 1997 study "Motherhood Today: A Tougher Job, Less Ably Done," The Pew Center for The People and The Press found that only 29 percent of the American women surveyed believe that when both parents work full-time they can do a good job of child raising. "Women, whether or not they work, believe the more traditional setting, in which the father works full-time and the mother stays home, is best for raising children, the survey reported."[5]

The bottom line: This is a personal choice, and not an easy decision, especially for women who have been fast-tracking since the teen years, climbing the ladder of success and deriving great satisfaction and an increased sense of self-worth for a job well done. Hearing the not-so-subtle media message promoting full-time work, some young women approach motherhood as just another item on the to-do list of accomplishments: college, check. Grad school, check. Good job with title, check. Decent apartment, great wardrobe, check. Better job, check. Nice vacation, check. Marriage, check. First condo or house, check. Baby, check—or so it seems. Child care, popular culture tells her, is a decision on a par with whether to nurse or bottle-feed.

Many women we talked to had originally subscribed to the notion that they could do it all and have it all, and proceeded accordingly. Liz Laufer, a Harvard Law School graduate, thought she had it all worked out: a great job in the U.S. Attorney's office and her mother to care for the baby in her home just outside of Silicon Valley. Her colleagues took bets on how long a maternity leave this hard-driving attorney would take. Two weeks was the average guess. Liz, now forty and the mother of two sons, ages nine and six, never returned. But trading a rush hour commute in the morning for pushing a stroller in the afternoon was not an easy transition. "The birth of my first child was very much an epiphany," says Liz. "I was very much a workaholic and worked up to the end of pregnancy. When Ben was born I fell so in love that I couldn't leave him. It was a combination

116

of emotional need and a physical aching to be with him. The feelings threw me into an existential crisis because, if I was to stay home, I needed to forge a new identity not based on being a trial lawyer. Every day for two years I mulled it over. Although I was blissful with him, I had also spent all those years developing a career. I kept telling myself that I would go back." What crystallized the choice for Liz was a speaker at a women's luncheon who preached the postfeminist mothering maxim: "You can have it all but not necessarily all at the same time." Liz now works part-time giving lectures, consulting, and helping with litigation. Most of her time, though, is spent, as she describes it, "experiencing childhood with kids, having adventures, driving them to lessons, answering their questions, calming their concerns, playing with them. Nine years later I am certain I made the right choice."

Why does a married, educated, middle-class woman approach the childbearing years with the assumption that full-time work is the only road to take? Part of the thinking comes from within herself as a result of the intellectual, emotional, and financial rewards of a career. However, another part stems from the cultural propaganda that a woman is shortchanging herself if she alters her career commitment for her children. To do otherwise is to betray all women who blazed the trail before her. In fact, a mythology of sorts—let's call them "new wives' tales"—has developed around why women should choose not to stay at home. With a nod to David Letterman, here's our top ten list of new wives' tales, with comments from stay-at-home moms around the country. We'll start with myth number ten.

Myth #10: You can't afford to stay at home

Admittedly for many families there is no choice; both parents must work to provide the basic necessities in life. Beyond a certain income level, however, the basic necessities can mean more than mortgage payments, food, clothes, and transportation. Is a fly-drive vacation a necessity? Is dinner out several times a week a necessity? Those are questions a husband and wife must answer when trying to decide whether they can "afford" to live on one salary. More important, they must decide what their priorities are as a couple. The adjustment from two people living on two salaries to three people living on one salary is often financially and emotionally difficult for both husbands and wives. "At times, my husband laments losing the safety net my working provided. I'm the one who seems to miss the salary!" says Karen Slora, forty-three, from Chicago, who worked for ten years as an industrial psychologist. "When I quit my paid job, our household income decreased by half!" How have they managed? Karen explains, "We have cut back in some areas and have 'simplified' our lives overall. This has been a good thing for us. It's also been good for the kids to see that more toys are not necessarily better and to see us talk about the cost of various things."

Despite the strain, many couples are willing to put all their economic eggs in one basket because of their shared vision of their family life. "Money was never an issue," says Josephina Cervantes, thirty-four, of Littleton, Colorado. "For some time my husband and I had been looking at quality-of-life issues. When we would both travel, either alternating weeks or whatnot, we realized that we were not living a good quality of life and that we just weren't keeping up with our lives, our family, our finances, our house. Anything!" says

Josephina. Her career had been marked by one success after another. When her daughter was born, Josephina worked as a telecommunications consultant in Mexico and finished up her M.B.A. For a year she commuted back and forth between Colorado and Mexico while her daughter was cared for at a day-care center. She hoped that the M.B.A. would lead to a teaching job, but instead it brought her an offer—which she accepted—of an executive-level job with a six-figure salary at a cable company.

A miscarriage and then another pregnancy forced her to rethink her decision to continue working. Josephina recalls, "It was very difficult to let go. I had a very powerful position. I was an executive. I had a lot of respect. I had people reporting to me. I had responsibilities for profit and loss. It was an exciting industry. Obviously I had risen to the executive ranks in a very short time and I was thinking, 'Okay, so this is what it's all about: The higher up you go, the less you see your family and your children, the more headaches you have with your staff with the politics?' And I thought, 'No thank you.' It did take me two or three months to grieve over having left that position."

A year later, Josephina has formed a new circle of friends—other mothers who have made the same decision. Many of them have a difficult time making ends meet and work part-time to earn spending money. She and her husband can withstand the financial crunch because they didn't marry until they were both thirty and had accumulated a nest egg. Still, Josephina says, "I'm more cognizant of what I spend now." But there are no regrets: "My whole family is happier and more stable. We live a simple, happy life. I can step back and smell the flowers."

Myth #9: You quit, defeated by the work-home juggling act

What Josephina and other women emphasize is that they made a *choice* to leave the legions in full-time work. We found that several common scenarios can lead to that decision. For some women, the impending birth of a second child triggered a rethinking of the family's lifestyle. One child is manageable for many women who want to continue working, especially if they have good child care. But as baby grows and expands his or her universe, it becomes more difficult to manage a schedule that often includes play dates, preschool, library hours, and sports. Add a second child and it takes incredible organizational skills and superhuman energy. Women don't retreat in defeat to the home front—they march on in victory with new worlds to conquer.

We found this was particularly true with first-time moms over the age of thirty. An attitude of "been-there-done-that" prevailed. They had worked, many for ten years or more, proven they could succeed in their careers, and were now ready for new challenges that had nothing to do with what their resumes said. Many women also had a sense of perspective, tempered by the opinion of people they admire.

Echoing a common sentiment, Marian Gormley, forty-three, of Falls Church, Virginia, says, "What helped was one thing my dad always said when I was trying to make a decision: 'What is going to matter in ten years?' It's not going to matter in ten years if I didn't debug software. It will matter that I wasn't here for my children. In that respect, we are basically choosing to live our priorities."

Some women even plan in advance—of marriage in many cases—not to ride the child-work merry-go-round.

The reasons vary, but many cited their own upbringing. Some grew up with stay-home moms and they wanted to re-create that family life; others grew up with working moms—among the first feminists—who had been overly stressed by career and family.

Other women had observed too many coworkers with harried lives. Patty Larson, thirty-nine, of Chicago, had worked eleven years as a customer service manager and four years as a technical writer and trainer. She and her husband had hiked in Hawaii and visited China before they became parents, knowing such vacations would later be unlikely. One Friday afternoon three years ago, she finished work, went into labor on the following Monday, and by midweek was an at-home mom. "I knew ahead of time that I would quit my job to stay home with my daughter," she says. "My husband and I decided it was very important that one of us stay home. I've seen too many parents looking frazzled and not giving their full attention to either work or family. Usually the family gets shortchanged. I feel that family should come first. Also, why have a family if you can't be there for them and enjoy them?"

Patty and many other women find that the economic and emotional adjustment to staying home is considerably smoother if baby is part of a long-term plan. Says Patty, "I have an M.B.A. in operations management. My education got me to the point, financially and mentally, where I could quit and stay home full-time."

Myth #8: The drudgery factor

All you do is cook, clean, and do laundry, over and over. It's like shoveling sand into the ocean. You spend your life doing chores, running errands, and carpooling. You have no time for yourself, according to yet another new wives' tale. There's no doubt that there's a certain amount of drudgery in caring for a family and home. Yet there's also a sense of freedom to set your own pace and hours, to farm out what you can afford, to ignore what you choose, and to do the rest in whatever manner suits your temperament. Not every house has a floor clean enough to eat off. That's not the reason for quitting a rewarding job. Instead, what attracts so many women could be called the "pleasures of home."

"Like any job there are moments it is very boring and frustrating; at other times I feel incredibly fulfilled using my skills," says Karen Slora. She tried everything from part-time work to maternity leave before she decided, as she began her second pregnancy, that it was time to stay home for a few years. To her surprise she discovered many unexpected joys. "The pleasures of being home involve the pleasure of being there for the kids," she says. "When they have a question, I'm there. When they are hurt, I'm there. Importantly, when they want to know more about sex or God, I am also there. I feel like we are instilling our values in our children. I also hope that we are developing a solid relationship for the future, with a strong emotional connection. When one is not rushing from one activity to another, the days 'unfold' in a beautiful way and have a rhythm all their own.

"So the morning might be spent doing chores as the kids watch TV, draw, read, or play with friends. And the afternoons might find us swimming, or with easels set up in our driveway, or setting up a lemonade stand. Even with the demands of preschool, classes, and kindergarten, there are large chunks of time when we just 'are.' The days 'flow,' and that is what makes my staying at home seem so right."

Small children force many women to slow down for the first time in their adult lives and to see life from a perspective of about three feet off the ground. Jennifer Ransdell, thirty-four, of Chicago, was convinced that she would be "miserable at home." She continued that thinking through her maternity leave until the time came to return to work. As her son's first birthday approached, she realized that day care was not a choice for her. Now she delights in life with her two small children. She recounts: "I am awakened each morning with a kiss by my children and a gentle 'Good morning, Mommy!' Many mornings we start our day by reading a book and eating breakfast, talking about any dreams we remember and what the plan is for the day. I get to plan my life. If I feel like I want to just lie in the grass and look at the clouds, that is what we do. I get to enjoy morning thunderstorms, cuddling in bed with my kids. There are days when I get dressed just because I want to, not because I have to. I have not had to wear panty hose in years—well, except for the occasional funeral or wedding. I have learned more about pirate ships, castles, and hot air balloons than I ever dreamed. I get to be in a play group! I rarely have to rush to make dinner so I'm not eating at 9:00 P.M. I can spend the whole morning at the library. I can go to the zoo and not have to deal with a crowd. I rarely have to wait in a line longer than the checkout at the grocery store. I get to shop all the sales that start on Friday morning and not have to fight over the last Wonderbra."

Myth #7: Your mind turns to mush

The "mush" myth holds that mothers at home are isolated, without any adult conversation or intellectual stimulation. One sociologist even warned that husbands eventually find their stay-home wives boring because they no longer share their exploits in the working world! There's no question that caring for an infant can seem like quarantine to new mothers. But as the round-the-clock schedule settles into a routine of eating, burping, and regular naps, most women look beyond the diapers and realize there are other people out there just like them. Yes, conversation may revolve initially around baby food, but it quickly moves into discussions of on-line investing, housing costs, taxes, exercise, the latest movies, and celebrity gossip—the same banter heard around the office water cooler. "Any mother who doesn't get adult stimulation can only blame herself," says Jennifer. "I have the most interesting, intelligent conversations with moms in my kids' playgroup, people I meet at the park, and in the store. Whenever I feel a little lonely, there is always the phone. There are newspapers and books to read and talk radio to listen to. When I had my first child, I was very lonely and felt very isolated. I forced myself to contact other mothers. We started to meet at each other's houses and have lunch together. Most of these moms have a college education. If you get a college education and never work at all in your field, the education is not wasted."

Karen hasn't lost the intellectual curiosity that prompted her to earn a Ph.D. "The adult stimulation comes through networking over time and pursuing your interests," she says. "If you were to sit in your office all day and never join any associations or attend professional meetings, chances are you would not grow professionally and you would feel isolated in your work environment. The same holds for stay-at-home mothering. Regarding the stimulation, it depends on how you choose to spend your spare time. I wanted to learn more about finances, so I joined an investment club. This is work I can do at my discretion. My interest in book reading has been rekindled by my joining a local book club. These are all activities I can easily do at home in small installments of time."

Not only does a woman's mind not turn to mush, she develops new ways of seeing, and not only through her children's eyes. After years of crashing head-on into life and all its challenges, women find breathing space and the time to reflect while at home. The delight that little things can bring was recaptured for Jennifer Ransdell when she spent one early summer day building sand castles on a deserted beach with her children. "It was the first real sand castle I had built since I was a girl. We had so much fun, and I was able to concentrate only on having fun. I have a lot more time to think about life and relationships and have realized that in life you have to deal with realities and not with an ideal that doesn't exist. I have rethought my priorities, and now I understand why mothers have always been stereotyped as being selfless and giving. They have to be. I cannot imagine not being able to help take care of the people I love. That is what being a mother and a wife is about. That is my job."

Karen too has found that she has changed in the four years that she has been at home. "Perhaps the major change I can see is that I tend to be much more people-focused, and I have become more relationship-oriented. Also, I have developed a tremendous capacity to juggle many different tasks. As some days I only have five-minute allotments in which to get things done, I find I do the work much more efficiently. I am also more comfortable with having many projects in the air. I've developed a domestic side that I never had and am proud that I have made a home for my family. What I get back, besides fatigue and sometimes feeling very emotionally 'stretched,' is knowing that I am being the best I can be for my family. I'm finding humor in the mundane acts of life, and I laugh at myself more. I'm expressing my creativity in various ways, from making crafts (something I thought I would never do!) to keeping a family journal. I feel more well rounded and that *this* is the essence of life, right here, snuggling with my six-year-old and nursing my toddler, or reading books with them. There is something very basic to being at home, and I am glad I didn't overlook the hidden treasures of the wonderful mundane moments."

Myth #6: Staying home is a sacrifice

Sacrifice is a loaded word. It implies suffering and hardship and that you're giving up something wonderful for something that's only so-so. Oddly, the people who view staying at home as a terrible sacrifice are often on the outside, peeping in the kitchen window, not on the inside, looking out. The women we talked to were honest in their assessment. Marian Gormley, the Falls Church, Virginia, mother of ten-year-old twins, admits, "Daily I make sacrifices for my family. I don't do housework joyfully. I wasn't one of those women who couldn't wait to have a home, to cook and do laundry. But I do it happily because it has to be done. I choose not to dwell on the housework; instead I think how fortunate I am to be at home." She realizes too that she's not the only one making concessions in her lifestyle. "My husband has to travel and he feels it's a deep infringement on his family life, but he does that because this is the job that provides for our family. He makes a sacrifice not requesting me to work full-time. The full financial burden falls on him, but he has embraced that role."

Many mothers view staying home as a trade-up rather than a trade-off. Karen brings a sense of perspective to her view: "Time comes and goes once, and there is only one chance to raise my family. Now I have no work-family conflict. My family is my work. If the kids are sick, there is no frantic calling of clients, relaying of project status to coworkers, etcetera. My personal schedule is impacted, but no harm is done. The hectic morning rush of scrambling out the door and the late nights looking over client reports when the kids are asleep are over. And I see and talk to my husband now."

Speaking of husbands, why not Mr. Mom? Movies aside, it seems that the stay-home dad is not a popular notion with either men or employers. Despite many companies that offer flextime and paternity leave, only a small percentage of men take advantage of them. The reasons why could easily fill another book. Some men are unwilling, some men simply can't take time off from their careers, and some men perceive that the business world gives only lip service to paternity leave. That's not to say that husbands don't help. They take kids to the park and to sports activities. Some even pick up the dry cleaning *and* do the grocery shopping. Ask for more and many men need a spreadsheet to coordinate the activities. Women on the other hand multitask like crazy.

The truth is that many women stay home because they want to. No one—husband, children, or society—is forcing them into this decision. Jennifer Ransdell explains, "I give my family stability. They always know where I am and that I am available at a moment's notice. I give my husband peace of mind. I get an endless supply of love and the joy of watching the kids grow, intellectually and physically. I have peace of mind knowing that I am doing the absolute best for my children. I have summers at the park and the beach, I have winters sledding and in museums, and I can go shopping almost whenever I want—as long as it isn't too close to nap time. I get to do what I love to do—teach and take care of the people I love."

Myth #5: Your marriage will suffer

A couple does not go from two careers and living in the fast lane to Dad, Mom, and Baby at home on one salary without some bumps in the road. Those early, sleepless nights can strain the most secure marriage. There is a period of realignment when both husband and wife have to adjust to the new living conditions. Marian Gormley, who was told at twenty-seven she could never have children only to have twins at age thirty-two, recalls, "I initially felt that my husband wanted a lovely clean house and children with hands folded welcoming Dad to a gourmet dinner. It was a struggle for us to get beyond his unrealistic expectations and mine too. I had been the best software engineer I could be. I wanted the same at home—to be the best wife and mother I could be, so I tried becoming supermom and superwife. I, too, felt I should make gourmet dinners even though I had twins. It was a struggle at first to view each other as equal partners. I thought he had the easy way out with travel and expense-account meals at nice restaurants. He thought I had the easy way with no clients and bosses or work pressures. We had to talk about it. We had to learn to appreciate each other's role. We had to help each other realize how important our respective roles were. Personally, I had to learn all that myself."

Eventually new rhythms and patterns are established. Life evens out only if the wife is happy with her decision to be home—and clear about her reasons—and if her husband is engaged with their children and doesn't see them as the mother's responsibility alone. Many women find their married life enriched. "We now rely on each other much more," says Shannon Purushothaman, thirty, an Atlanta mother of two children. "Before the children it almost seemed like we were two single people sharing a life together. After our first child and then our second, it took mutual trust and reliance to be able to care for them. At times the chaos of two small children is stressful. However, it makes us more dependent on each other. We need the other's support to be able to survive all the normal childhood stresses that occur."

Although it might not be politically correct to admit it, many women, especially those who see married life as a joint venture, get emotional satisfaction because they can lessen their husbands' stress levels. "I would say my marriage is stronger now," says Karen. "Our lifestyle, although still hectic with two young children, is not as harried as it would be if I were working. My husband and I are able to share many moments together, often with the family, which would not have been possible. We have developed a 'team' approach over the years and have decided that these roles work best for our 'team' for now. However, I think what helps him is knowing that the kids are being taken care of by their mother, the woman who shares his values. He does not have to worry about their caretaker or getting a call saying the kid is running a fever so could you pick her up now? Events on the home front are handled as they arise so he can better concentrate on his work."

Some women even feel they help their husbands do their jobs better, and that benefits the whole family. Before she married, Jennifer Boutte, who worked as an environmental engineer in Texas, discussed child-rearing with her boyfriend. Both believed that one parent needed to be home and agreed that her career would be secondary for the first ten years of their marriage. At the decade mark, she says, "We will reevaluate that decision to determine whether or not we will continue to stand behind his career or if my career choice will dominate." Now seven years into that plan, she is pleased with her decision and feels that she is an "integral part" of her husband's success. "My being home allows him to concentrate on work while he's at work," Jennifer says. "He knows I have most things under control at home. He doesn't have to worry about our child getting sick and whether or not he's going to have to take some days off because he knows I'll be here. I think the main thing is he can concentrate on what he needs to do at work to be successful."

Myth #4: Quality time is better than quantity time

Working mothers who don't spend a great quantity of time with their children contend they share quality time with them, which is even better. They float images of serene mothers sitting crossed-legged on the floor with children, playing with puzzles, reading piles of books, and creating impressionistic finger paintings. That's quality time for working mothers. Quality time for at-home moms is often presented as wasted, with mothers doing laundry while children sit parked in front of the TV. One of the weapons in the mommy wars are studies that claim to prove that working mothers spend more quality time with children than stay-home mothers. Studies, of course, can be skewed for the desired result. What matters is that many women are convinced that both quality and quantity time are critical. Quality time, many mothers will tell you, is not something you can schedule. "It assumes everyone is ready for the 'quality moment' at the same time," says industrial psychologist Karen Slora. "Given kids' fussy moods and adults' frustrations, it is difficult to schedule an optimal time. I find that quality moments occur most often on those days I am spending 'quantity' time. I may feel hassled, but then I look over and I see my girls playing dress-up, inviting me to their tea. Or they ask for a book-reading marathon. These are spur-of-the-moment events that cannot be scheduled. Try postponing those moments and the kids are no longer interested."

Many mothers also believe that quality time does not revolve around only play. It happens when children ask those seemingly innocent questions that form the core of their attitudes, opinions, and beliefs. Children don't save the important questions for bedtime. "We provide our children with our philosophies and beliefs and those may be completely different from those espoused by that child-care provider, even if they know baby massage and have passed the infant CPR class," says Jennifer Ransdell. "Children are sponges, and even an off-chance remark can stay with them forever. There have been many occasions when they will bring up something that I didn't even think they heard. I cannot imagine what seemingly innocent comments they could be soaking up by having their quantity time spent with someone other than their parent."

That's exactly the reason that Marian still chooses to stay home, even though her ten-year-old twins are busy with their own lives. For her and many other mothers, the middle-school years are just as crucial as early childhood for daily, on-the-scene mothering. "I pull all the pieces together to make sure that the family's priorities are implemented in our daily lives," she says. "I make sure we try to live our values and virtues. I look around us in the world today and see that there are a lot of children who don't have an intimate relationship with parents. I'm able to pick up my children every day after school and hear firsthand the joys and challenges of what happened to each of them. I'm the one that's there to share the after-school snack, help with homework and studying for tests, chauffeur them to their sports practices and games, and cheer them on (sometimes too loudly!) from the sidelines. We have candlelight family dinners almost every night, have family movie night on Friday nights, and family game night on Sunday nights. As our children age, my husband and I realize this is critical: that day-to-day time consistency, that atmosphere, really makes a difference."

And for Patty, the quality vs. quantity time argument can be answered simply: "As someone once said, 'If a boss doesn't understand quality of time vs. quantity of time, how do we expect a child to understand?'"

Myth #3: You are committing economic suicide

Another common myth is that the balance of economic power tips in the husband's favor when the wife stays at home. That certainly may have been true decades ago. Then a woman went directly from her parents' home to her husband's home with little college or career in between. Many women had no idea what their family income or assets were; they didn't write the checks or pay the bills. However, today's family CEO is in a much better position to protect herself financially. In many cases, she not only pays the bills and hires the contractor, she also plans for the college savings and retirement accounts. She has charge accounts in her name and established credit before getting married. "I know what all of our assets are, and I have access to all of our assets," says Jennifer Boutte. "I also know that I can take care of myself if I need to. I did it before I got married, and I am certain I could do it again."

Many of the women we talked with were emphatic that they could support themselves if they needed to because they've stayed connected to the work world. "How you keep yourself active as a stay-at-home mother—i.e., through networking with other moms and skills attained from volunteering—can be very advantageous in trying to return to work," says Shannon. She argues that this issue should be moot if husband and wife approach marriage as equal partners. "Once again this brings the point home of marrying the 'right' person," she adds. The "right" person is the husband who views his paycheck as the family paycheck, who views his wife's contributions at home as valuable as his at work. Both husband and wife come out winners. "I allow my husband the freedom to do what he needs to do in his work. And I have discovered how loving and supportive he is to me and our children, " Shannon says.

Some women agree with the "economic suicide" theory but argue that the at-home life is worth the gamble. "A woman who has stayed at home to raise her children and is left by her husband has committed economic suicide," says Jennifer Ransdell. "She has also committed emotional suicide. So what! Life is a risk. If you're going to live your life by thinking of what might happen, you will never do anything. No one has a crystal ball. Life happens. It is your duty to do what is right while it is happening. Somehow you will survive. It may not be easy or fun, but at least you will be asking, 'Would you like fries with that?' knowing that you did your best for your children."

Myth #2: Stay-at-home moms don't contribute to society

There's an attitude sometimes whispered that stay-at-home moms are a drain on society's resources. They took someone's seat at college or in a job and now they've given it up. Sure they help fuel the economy with all those sneakers and soccer balls, but do they really contribute anything substantial for the good of society as a whole? Absolutely. Just listen to Karen. Instead of using her Ph.D. to help a company with human-resources problems, she has turned her attention to her community. "I have found that I genuinely care about our neighborhood and local events," she says. "Being at home most of the day has made my residential community that much more important to me. And us stay-at-home moms are the ones who notice the streetlights not working, the manhole covers not placed properly, the repeat speeders, etcetera. I find I read the local paper now with greater interest than ever before, because I can see the impact of town politics on our corner of the world more clearly."

Liz cites her California community as an example. "In my immediate circle of friends, there are highly educated women with graduate degrees and they run the local schools like a business. They bring professionalism to all sorts of volunteer organizations." That's the story across the country as high-powered women get involved with community organizations large and small.

And, the number one new wives' tale . . .

Myth #1: The stay-at-home mom stays home

The number one myth about stay-at-home moms is that they're stuck in the house. Nothing could be further from the truth. As Marian says, "My mother was a stay-home mom and she was *really* at home—and very happily too. That's not true of many of the stay-home moms of today. I volunteer for Girl Scouts and at the children's school. The children are involved in many sports and activities. I work part-time doing public relations from home. I don't feel stuck anywhere. I've chosen this lifestyle."

It's time for a new nomenclature. Don't ring their doorbells. They are just not at home anymore.

———◆———

The degree to which these new wives' tales affect the decision to stay home varies greatly from woman to woman. However, one compelling reason for staying home, emphasized by all the women we talked to, is the danger of life in contemporary America. Gone are the days when kids could play in pajamas on the street on summer nights; gone are the days when the schoolyard was a safe haven. Working parents are getting a harsh wake-up call, and it's not from their side-by-side alarm clocks. It is the frightening sound of gunfire heard in a school library in Littleton, Colorado, and in the commons room in a Conyers, Georgia, high school. On the heels of these horrific acts, it's no surprise that more and more mothers feel a gravitational pull to stay at home, in the hope that on-the-spot parenting will check antisocial and aggressive behavior at its earliest moment as well as protect their children. Liz, the former U.S. Attorney, knows of what she speaks. "Today society is much more dangerous for children. It's more violent and creates stresses for children that weren't there when we were growing up. It is horrendous that we can't safely let our children experience some of the greatest joys of childhood such as riding their bikes up and down the street. We need to supervise them constantly."

And it's not only parents who are frightened. A Nickelodeon/Yankelovich survey found that an alarming 31 percent of children aged twelve to seventeen knew someone in their age group who carried a gun. And 36 percent of children aged nine to seventeen worried about being attacked or beaten up at school.[6] Is it any wonder that parents no longer believe that schools are safe? How can they go off to work feeling confident that their children are not in harm's way? The National Association for the Education of Young Children and the American Psychological Association issued a joint, in-your-face op-ed statement emphasizing community attempts to make schools safer but advocating that efforts must start with parents and caretakers, long before youngsters reach the schools: "Violence can be prevented, starting with the youngest of our children; as parents and caregivers, we play a powerful role in this task, and there are specific, practical skills we can use. Very young children can learn effective ways for resolving anger, frustration, and conflict when they are surrounded by constructive role models, when they are taught to solve problems without violence, and when they are encouraged to share and to understand the feelings of others. Research shows that most violent behavior is learned, and the most profound and lasting 'lessons' in violence are learned in early life."[7]

At a backyard picnic, Marcia Kirschenbaum, a twenty-year veteran middle-school teacher in an affluent Long Island suburb, talked about how the role of schools changed in just the last year. "We're told to provide this nurturing environment in which children really want to learn. They certainly can't have that with a metal detector. You can't have that with a policeman at the front door. You can't have their book bags plastic and see-through and call that nurturing. Yet because we have children who are phoning in these fake threats and leaving these messages etched in their desks that a bomb is going off, we're in this horrible situation. We want to make it nurturing, but we also want to make it safe."

The situation today makes it all that more important for a parent—typically the mother—to be present and accounted for, and willing to participate in a child's life with more than just a 3:00 P.M. phone call from the office. "I don't care how many children say, 'It's okay, Mom, that you can't come.' It's really not okay," says Marcia. "Also kids need to be encouraged to share their feelings. If there is no one at home to share them with when they come home, when they're feeling the most of whatever they're feeling, what are they going to do with these feelings? Share them with the nanny? The housekeeper? And many of them are latchkey."

Clearly, the decision to stay home is not an easy one with both personal and societal pressures to consider. Weighing the pros and cons, Becky Goodell, thirty-four, a *Fortune* 500 management consultant, seems to have found a good balance for now, working part-time and caring for her three-year-old son, Danny. In 1998 her husband decided to quit a traditional law practice in Washington, DC, and work in Hollywood, negotiating deals for writers and producers. The new job meant Becky had to leave good friends, coworkers, and her only sibling, Susannah, on the East Coast. Fortunately, her employer in Washington offered her a three-day-week position in L.A. Everything should be perfect, but Becky is still "conflicted." She grew up in Muncie, Indiana, with a traditional family lifestyle. "My mom picked me up from school every day in high school; she baked homemade cookies every day. My mom was my best friend. I loved high school; it was not a troubling time like most people say. I was not a difficult teenager. I want to be able to do that for my children because that shaped me, and I think it kept me out of trouble. When Danny's in school, I want to be able to take him and pick him every day. That's my goal, because I feel like the older they get, the more important it is for you to be there, the more risks there are in our society. But at the same time, working outside the home is also important to my happiness."

Becky, trying to sort out her feelings, told her mother, Dottie, of our conversation. The conversation started sixty-five-year-old Dottie Goodell thinking about her life, and she shared her thoughts with us. Here's her reflection about the choices and change her daughter must face.

Dear Loretta and Mary,

I will try and answer what you have asked to the best of my ability, and hope it will give you another viewpoint that is probably now considered old-fashioned.

My husband, Charles, and I were married one year after I finished college. I was an elementary schoolteacher and he a third-year medical student, eventually becoming a neurosurgeon after fourteen years in total training. Those were physically and financially tough years, but the greatest joy of our marriage came with the birth of our two daughters. Once the girls arrived, both of us felt I needed to be with them. It was not a problem, since it was where I wanted to be. For my husband and me, "liberation" truly meant I could stay home and be the one who raised the girls. Our generation followed such defined pathways that doing otherwise would have been strange. We instinctively knew our roles in society, and no one seemed to question any of it. It must have meant frustration and disappointment for many women, but I was not one of them. Our youngest daughter, Becky, who now has a child, realizes that what the women of my generation did is often not possible in today's economic climate where two incomes are needed to survive. She now understands I was able to stay at home and wanted to be at home. Everyone in my strata was doing exactly what I was doing.

Since I had always loved children and teaching, it seemed only natural that I would be the one to raise and teach my own. It was truly a labor of love and commitment. My husband was much too busy in his job of medicine, and although he was there if we needed him, the day-to-day raising of the girls was left to me. I thought then as I do now, I had the most important job in the entire world. I still feel that way, even in today's complicated environment where children are raised in all sorts of fashions. People now make fun of the times and the Father Knows Best theory of child-rearing, but it did appear to produce better results than we are now seeing with our youth of today who are so conflicted in a complicated world. Even the animal world takes care of its young. Present-day society is not looking after its children, and it is sad for all of us and for the future of our country.

I had always hoped when our daughters came of age, they would have careers, and then follow in the traditional role of "wife and mother." I am happy so many choices are available to them that were not available to us. Each generation is shaped by the times they live in, and I respect that. Whatever choices my daughters make I know *will be carefully thought out, for they are thoughtful people who are making their way in a world that is different from what I knew. Liberation for them has an entirely different message for their times. Nothing is ideal, and good and bad come from both sides of the aisle. I would not begin to judge. I just know that what we did seemed to produce better results than those we are now seeing. Children are resilient, and they are surviving, but at a great cost for many of them. I do not pretend to know what the answers are in this matter, but I feel changes will have to take place for improvement, for we have reached a low level when our children are not safe in their own schools.*

And the beat goes on . . . Our children constantly provide us with great activities and pleasure. They are still our best friends, and we look forward to the times when we are together. Our grandson, Danny, is an extra bonus of parenthood and the joy of all of our lives.

Sincerely,
Dottie Goodell

ᕲ What Message Are We Sending? ᕲ

More than one mother mentioned to us that she wondered what message she was sending to her daughters by staying home. Will her little girl think that only women do chores and only men go to work? What we found fascinating about this query is that the women who asked this question all were doing substantial part-time work—paid or volunteer—and their husbands all "helped out" . . . a lot! Why is it that even when convinced that we have made the right choice to stay home—now, at this point in our lives—we still have a little voice nagging: work full-time, pull out the suits, pantyhose and pumps?

We answer the question about the message we may be sending to our daughters with a question of our own: What message are we sending by living a frenzied life, by barely finding quiet moments to talk to our husbands, by gasping to find free time with children, by not having a moment to ourselves? Is *that* the image we want to send to our daughters?

We don't pretend to have all of the answers. One answer that seems to ring true with us and with the women who shared their feelings with us is the oft-repeated "do it all, just at different times." And that's what we tell our daughters. Look for a career that's flexible, that can be reinvented again and again. Don't be afraid to take risks. Don't let society dictate how you should live your life. Those are the messages that we hope we are sending.

What we also shouldn't forget is that our message to our sons is equally important: We hope that you will marry a woman who is your partner and your soul mate, and that you will give her all the love and support *she* deserves.

5

Learning the Art of Coping... for Better or for Worse

MARRIAGE IS FILLED with memory-making moments, from the honeymoon, to the first child, to the twenty-fifth anniversary trip. But along with the peaks come the valleys. It's unavoidable: troubles with children, money, in-laws, jobs. The effect of a crisis can either drive a wedge or foster an increased intimacy between a couple. What makes the difference? The women we talked to said they were able to weather difficulties because of their partnership approach to marriage as well as their commitment—and their husbands' commitment—to a long-term relationship. In our own marriages, Mary's husband, Frank, calls it having a soul mate; Loretta's husband, Vic, calls it having a best friend. Many women echoed those words in describing their relationship with their husbands.

The new traditional wife seems to have a particular ability to cope with a crisis. It's a quality they all share. Perhaps it's a personality trait, perhaps it's a philosophy of life; we won't attempt to psychoanalyze them. Instead we'll let the stories speak for themselves. That's not to say that coping is easy. All marriages have rough spots, and sometimes the wife feels she is carrying the load alone. Being a supportive wife does not mean always wearing a Colgate smile. Our coping mechanisms are sometimes counterbalanced by feelings of anxiety, frustration, and loneliness.

Several women we spoke with were incredibly candid about how they survived trying circumstances and how they got through the difficult times. Not so coincidentally, some of these women are married to well-known men. Perhaps they were more forthcoming than most because, at one time or another, the media has examined their husbands' lives with varying degrees of intensity. While their individual experiences may be unique, their emotions and reactions are universal.

Take Anna Romano: husband Ray's *Everybody Loves Raymond* sitcom is a prime-time hit. Only a few years ago, Ray, a struggling stand-up comic, and Anna, an administrative assistant turned full-time mom, were living in a blue-collar suburb of New York City. When Ray got a shot at his own television program, Anna, with three kids and one more on the way, was less than eager to pick up and move to Los Angeles, a place as strange to her as Timbuktu. But Anna, too, loves Raymond, and she agreed to make the move—after the show was renewed for a full season. And other wives, not in the public eye, will also attest that moving for your husband's career is one of the hallmarks of a supportive wife.

When Ellen Hart Peña's husband, Federico, was tapped by Bill Clinton as secretary of transportation, Ellen agreed to leave Denver for the fishbowl of Washington, DC. It didn't take long for her personal demons to be dragged through the Washington press. Then there is Norris Mailer who has carefully navigated life as the wife of twentieth-century literary icon Norman Mailer. Norris has juggled her career, children, and a hungry media, always looking for a morsel from the Mailers. Cookie Johnson learned the meaning of "for better or for worse" in 1991 when her husband, Magic, announced to the world that he was HIV positive. Cookie stood by his side looking stoic and courageous, and discovered how to find good in a bad situation. Loyita Woods married actor Bob Woods, but fertility problems tested the strength of their commitment. Anna, Ellen, Norris, Cookie, and Loyita all chose to be supportive wives; they were all tested—in public—and managed to cope and more than hold their ground.

∾ Coping . . . with a Big Move ∾

Moving is one of life's major stresses, right up there with health problems or a new baby.[1] The changes are only beginning after the boxes are unpacked. There are myriad adjustments, from finding a jogging trail to making new friends.

Our routines are upset, the familiar is unfamiliar. For a single man or woman, the move can be an adventure. For a couple with kids, it can be one of life's most stressful situations.

Anna Romano encouraged her husband, Ray, to take a shot at starring in a fledgling sitcom for CBS when he was asked to sign on for six episodes. But she was not about to move from the familiar and familial surroundings of Middle Village, Queens, while Ray filmed in L.A. It was too risky; the show could be canceled after a week, and Ray could return to his job as a stand-up comic. So while Anna waited out the first season from August until March, Ray bunked in Beverly Hills with a writer friend, who happened to be single. Anna couldn't help being a little concerned. "I kept thinking his friend is trying to meet women and Ray is with him," Anna recalls. "I trust Ray totally. I would say, 'Ray, it may not be you, but women know who you are now. They want to be in the limelight. They know I'm not there.'"

The Romano scenario is not uncommon, according to Gary Klein, vice president and managing director of the media and entertainment practice at A. T. Kearney Executive Search. Klein often places people in jobs that require relocation. "The husband will go into the new opportunity and the wife and children will remain where they are," he says. "It will be a testing ground. The wife will say, 'Listen, before we take up and move, you should be sure that this is the right opportunity for the family. And we'll stay where we are and we'll see you on the weekend or every other weekend and we'll work it out.'"

It didn't take long for *Everybody Loves Raymond* to become a smash hit. Ray, Anna, and three children moved into a house in the San Fernando Valley, a family-friendly suburb. The move wasn't easy for Anna, from finding a new home, to getting the kids settled in schools, to dealing with an unexpected fourth Romano on the way. She describes her first days in L.A., "I was nauseous. The smell of the paint, the smell of stain on the wood floors. And it was 110 degrees."

Consider this: most women told us that their husbands were no-shows on moving day. Somehow husbands are not at home either when the moving truck arrives to be loaded at the old house or unloaded at the other end. Ray was no different; Anna managed the move herself. Fortunately, like many other wives, Anna had a support system in place. She called on Ray's mother—her parents are deceased—who has always been there for her and the kids. "Thank God she came, because we got here on a Monday night, and Tuesday Ray was off to work."

Once they were settled, there were still plenty of adjustments. Even little things like finding their favorite foods became a project. "There are a lot of differences and it's unusual because we're in the same country. I remember looking for Hellman's mayonnaise. It's called Best Foods in California. What is that?" she asks.

It wasn't only the food. Everything about the entertainment business seemed foreign to Anna. "I don't know anything. I'm still learning. It's like learning a new language." She also found that Ray's success carried a price of seemingly endless rehearsals and late-night rewrites. Wanting her kids to be with their dad more and to be comfortable with his business, she decided to bring them—one at a time—to the weekly tapings at the Burbank studio.

In a room designed as a play space for the kids in the cast, six-year-old Gregory shoots hoops into a kid-sized basketball stand while Anna shares her feelings about Ray's focus on his career.

Anna realizes that for now Ray must be fully committed to his show, leaving little time or energy for the family, and she totally supports him while he builds his career. "This is his first shot, his only shot," explains Anna. "He can't say, 'No.' I let him go do his thing. I feel almost like the show is the 'other woman,' because that's all he sleeps, thinks of, dreams or talks about."

Laughing, she adds, "By the end of the year I told Ray, 'If one more person tells me what a wonderful person you are, I'm going to kill them, and I'm going to kill you because last year was horrible.' Now I'm just used to it."

Ray jokes about his relationship with Anna in both his stand-up routines and in his 1998 bestseller, *Ray Romano: Everything and a Kite*. He writes, "While my business traveling lets me stay in hotels, sleep late, and even go golfing sometimes, it's important for me to remember that my wife is home running the household by herself. So, while I may occasionally have fun on the road, I try to keep in mind the most important thing: Don't let her know it."[2]

Anna's New York friends fantasize about her hobnobbing with the Hollywood set. "A friend of mine was e-mailing me. It was all questions. 'Do you have celebrity friends? Do you . . . ?' I'm sorry. I sound like a broken record but, no, I don't. I get up in the morning. I don't even shower. I take my kids to school. I do the same things I did in New York. I'm just doing them in California now."

When Anna finally breathed a sigh of relief, settling into a routine, even one with odd hours, the show went on break and Ray was off to New York to host *Saturday Night Live*. "That was a big thing for us. We were so excited. That's our hometown. It's funny, now that we live here, on hiatus he's in New York doing his job. I can't win," she says, shaking her head.

It takes quite a while to recover from those uncomfortable feelings of being a stranger in a strange land. Add that to the emotional and physical fatigue of setting up a new household and by the time we get to cuddle up in our new bed, we are numb. We would like to fall to pieces or kick and scream, but unfortunately, as wives and mothers, we rarely have the luxury of nursing our anxieties and exhaustion. Time just doesn't allow it. Nor do the kids.

Ellen Hart Peña certainly learned that lesson when it became her responsibility to orchestrate the move to Washington, DC, and make the unfamiliar familiar for her husband and their two daughters. Federico was already wrapped up in his new job as secretary of transportation. Although the move was unplanned, both agreed that he should not pass up the appointment. "Neither of us ever thought we'd be in Washington. Absolutely not," says Ellen. While Federico started his new job, Ellen put up the For Sale sign in the front yard in Denver and moved cross-country to a Washington, DC, apartment with two babies in tow—Nelly was two-and-a-half, and Cristina was not quite one.

The move was just part of the job for Ellen. A graduate of Harvard and the University of Colorado School of Law at Boulder, she views her role at this point in her life as the family's consummate caretaker. In a matter-of-fact way she rattles off her responsibilities: "Everything that is not [paid] work, I do. My kids do many activities including ballet and gymnastics. I am the person who picks them up and drives them to this activity and that activity."

An already difficult situation was made even harder two weeks after the move when her younger daughter was hospitalized for three days for an asthma attack and a vicious ear infection. The scene was surreal: new doctor, new town, no idea where the hospital was located, plus no babysitter and a husband unable to help because he was attending the president's first State of the Union address. Ellen recalls: "It was a cold and rainy winter day, really ugly, and I didn't know anybody. So Cristina is in the hospital, hooked up to the IV, we were looking up at the TV, and there was Federico at the president's address. Everything was completely unfamiliar. I also had Nelly with me and the head nurse came in to me with fire in her eyes and looked at Nelly and said, 'She can't be here.' I had no friends, no place to put her; I didn't know anyone. It had only been two weeks. And I said, 'Excuse me?' She kept saying she couldn't be here."

The next day, with Federico out of town, Ellen stopped at the supermarket on the way home from the hospital. "I'm trying to navigate traffic, and I had no idea where I was going. I'd given the little one a donut which she mashed into my hair," she says, still pained by the events. "We had $180 worth of food, and it fit fine when I had it in the cart. But after they bagged it up, it didn't fit. There were two extra bundles. The guy said, 'Pick up your groceries, ma'am.' I said, 'I really can't. I've got my hands full with the kids.' He looked at me and said, 'It's not my problem.' So I pushed the cart to the car and unloaded the groceries. The kids were crying. At this point, I just put my head on top of the car and started crying. And Nelly said, 'Mommy, I think you need a nap.'"

As in government, unbidden transfers are part of the deal in the corporate sector. Lila Lawler knows all about moving because she has relocated five times in the last twelve years—from Dallas to Princeton, to London, to Charlotte, to Annapolis. The first four moves were for her husband's job as a vice president of human resources for Pepsi; the last move was for a new position with another company. For this transfer, Lila, thirty-six, put together all the lessons she learned from the other moves. This transition was the smoothest for her and their two children, ages four and six. "This time, in Annapolis, we looked first for a neighborhood for the children and other people with common lifestyles rather than picking a house first," Lila explains. "In our Charlotte neighborhood we had a beautiful home on rolling hills. But the neighbors were older people, all very nice, but with very few little children and at a different point in their lives. This time we drove around looking for kids running outside, mothers pushing strollers, and swing sets in the backyard. We also chose a new development where other people were also new to the area and looking to make friends."

When we spoke to Lila, she was already hanging pictures on the wall, less than two weeks after she moved in. Not only does she have unpacking, putting up window treatments, and finding a new pediatrician down to a science, Lila also brings an "if you have a lemon, make lemonade" attitude to moving. "I think you have to look at moving as an adventure with new places to explore and new people to meet," she says.

Anne Moss, forty-two, of Warwick, New York, keeps a stack of "change of address" postcards handy because of her husband's career moves. As Jim has climbed the ladder as a newspaper publishing executive, the family has moved along with him—three times in ten years—from Manhattan to Miami, to mid-Pennsylvania, to upstate New York.

Married right out of college in 1978, Anne, based in the Big Apple, started building a name for herself, one click-of-the-camera and one film shoot at a time, on fashion runways and in feature films like Francis Ford Coppola's *Cotton Club.* "Jim and I had had a wonderful jet-set life," she says. "I had traveled all over the world . . . and he was traveling all the time . . . It was just an exciting and wonderful life."

Even the birth of their son in 1986 didn't slow her down. She cut back on the modeling and went into fashion-show production, where she often brought her baby to work. Even when her husband was offered an opportunity to work as assistant to the publisher of the *Miami Herald*, she saw a way to continue her career. No problem. If two years in Miami would be best for Jim's career, Anne would be "dual city." Since the fashion-show business is seasonal, Anne needed to be in Manhattan only a few weeks a year.

Within three days, she single-handedly sold their New York apartment, bought a Florida house, and prepared for the move. "He was on the fast track to become a newspaper publisher," she explains. "I thought I could have this life in Miami and this life in Manhattan and make it work." Yes, except that on the day she moved, Anne also found she was pregnant with her second child.

With that happy—and surprising news—Anne got the first inkling that maybe, just maybe, she and Jim couldn't both be fast-trackers. Something had to change in their lives, and it was her career. "My priorities shifted that day," she says. "I knew that from that point on, it would be about my being willing to make adjustments."

Still, Anne's can-do attitude prevailed even with the birth of her daughter. "I was adjusting now to life in Miami, far away from any support system." She managed to put together a part-time job as a model in TV and print commercials.

Then, almost two years to the day, a "once in a lifetime" opportunity came along—again. Anne recalls, "Jim walked in on Halloween and announced to me that we were moving to State College, Pennsylvania. I had a Domino's Pizza commercial running and a Ban Solid commercial running. I had all these wonderful things happening to me and then again here comes life thrown back up." This time, instead of a three-day advance notice, Jim was on the plane the next morning to take over as publisher of the *Centre Daily Times*.

Anne knew the drill and not only got the family settled but also took on the public role of publisher's wife, becoming active in local organizations. Despite those commitments, she was delighted when a local cable producer asked her to host a new talk show on women's basketball. With her community involvement, the television program, and her family, Anne was "playing" a full-court game, amazing her friends along the way. "I'm the CEO of our family," she says. "Our lives would not work without my organizational skills. You have to prioritize. You have to think things through; there has to be some coordination. I have a friend now who says, 'There's Anne with her alphabetized attic.'"

In 1996, the Mosses moved yet again (with advance notice this time) to a town about fifty miles north of New York City. Anne told us: "We thought this was the best of both worlds because we were within commuting distance to Manhattan. We had access to the arts and all the culture we could possibly want, and yet we still had the quality of life that we had while we were at State College." First, though, she had to get their lives in order—again! "To find doctors,

153

decorate the house, unpack all the boxes, get the kids in school and find all the programs that they need, find somebody to help you, find support systems you need, and so forth, it takes eighteen to twenty-four months."

The move also made it possible for her to consider resuming her professional life. Although Anne signed on with a Manhattan agent hoping to continue her career in broadcasting, she hasn't grabbed any offers. "What I am looking for is a way to continue to grow professionally and not sacrifice my family," she says. "I know that my happiness lies somewhere between the two extremes."

Two of the key questions we asked wives were: "Would you move for your husband's job?" and "Would he move for your job?" Despite the large number of women working, it's still the wives who usually move for their husbands, not the other way around. However, many corporations are increasingly aware that a wife might not be so willing to pull up roots, and indeed, sometimes refuses to do so. Executive search specialist Gary Klein recalls a situation that has become increasingly common after a job candidate negotiates a new position. "At the eleventh hour, the deal fell apart. When it became time to make that final decision, they couldn't do it because the wife felt that it just wasn't right, didn't feel good, didn't work, wasn't good for the kids, wasn't good for them," he says. "You try to avoid those situations up front by making sure they understand. 'Is this okay?' 'Have you discussed this with your spouse?'"

Adam Berkowitz fully discussed the possibility and implications of moving with his wife, Karen. It was her gentle shove that pushed him to accept an offer to move from New York City to L.A. The West Coast job offer for her husband was a strange turn of events for Karen. Before giving birth to their daughter, Natalie, it was Karen who struggled with the decision whether to make a cross-country move. She had worked for TriStar Pictures in New York but knew that the best opportunities for her were in Hollywood. "I thought about moving out to L.A. because I thought that was what was going to enhance my career," Karen told us. "I certainly would not leave when Adam was in New York and, by the time he was ready to make the move, I was already involved in my family. So I said, 'Isn't this sad? If it had been a few years before, I could have really furthered my career by being out in L.A.' But now, I've put my career aside to raise the family."

Karen, thirty-seven, the take-charge macro-manager, saw the big picture and convinced Adam that this was an important career move. "He credits me with everything we've done," Karen says. "I am the one that convinced him to do it. He was on the fence. Adam has such drive and ambition and always has. But to make a big move and to leave all his family was really a big thing because he is so close with his family. For me, that wasn't so hard. My family was already split up, but I was leaving my friends and my life. I was just getting settled with Natalie."

Karen did have some last-minute misgivings, admitting to Adam that she was scared when she realized the magnitude of the three-thousand-mile move. "You don't understand. We have to talk about it. You're just going to the same company. You've been to L.A. a million times. My whole life is changing."

It's been five years since their big move and there have been some surprises. Karen now loves living in Los Angeles with Adam and their two children, "It's like summertime all year round. My whole life has been enhanced. I now have made some of the best friends I have ever made in my life. It is so nice to meet women as an adult: You're the same now because you've all changed and evolved. I've met so many wonderful women through nursery school and through classes I take with the kids."

There's an irony here. Now that Karen is living in L.A, surrounded by movie industry people who could help her career, she has no intention of resuming it. "What is interesting is I'm not ready to go back to work yet. I'd like to have one more child. I want to wait until they are all well ensconced in school full time before I go back to work. I love taking them to their classes and coordinating their play dates, even though you feel like you're schlepping around so much. I relish my children and in a way, I feel almost more fulfilled as a person in raising my family."

⌒ Coping with . . . Your Life ⌒ on Public Display

Public life was familiar territory for Ellen and Federico Peña. Federico was mayor of Denver when he met and married Ellen, who quickly learned to be a good sport living in the limelight. She explains, "They want to know about your life and your marriage and what kind of dress you wore and about the kids. And most of that was just fine. They just felt part of our family and our lives. People seemed to respect our privacy. On the other side, they wouldn't hesitate to organize a protest on the front lawn."

The Denver spotlight was low voltage compared to the Klieg lights shined on bigwigs in Washington. It didn't take long for Ellen's past personal battle with bulimia and anorexia to become newspaper copy. It leaked when the manager of a U.S. running team asked Ellen to relate her intimate thoughts in a runner's newsletter. Ellen didn't hesitate. "I'd been an anorexic and bulimic for ten years and worked through some of the issues and had been healthy for five years," she says. "I tried out for both the '80 and '84 Olympic teams and was highly ranked in the 10 K. The newsletter editor knew about my problems and asked if I'd share some of my experience with her audience. It was much harder to put pen to paper than I expected, but I wrote something and I thought that was it."

The newsletter article led to a piece in *The Washington Post*. Then the story was picked up by *People* magazine, which gave the full treatment. While some may have been disconcerted by this very public exposure, Ellen saw it as an opportunity, a way to help others who were fighting similar battles with bulimia and anorexia. When a movie producer spotted Ellen's compelling story in *People*, he tracked her down and proposed making a movie-of-the-week, dramatizing her struggle with the illness and her journey to recovery.

"I had very specific reasons for wanting to do it. I felt, maybe out of naiveté, that I had a sense of trust in the people I dealt with, and that trust was completely borne out in the production company and the person from ABC," Ellen says. "I felt that they were committed to producing a piece that was balanced and not sensationalized and that communicated a sense of hope and recovery."

So the tables turned in the Peña household. Federico could have nixed the project, fearing political backlash. "He had severe misgivings because so much of our life is public, so what is private he guards preciously," Ellen says. The couple talked it through and Federico became "very supportive," so Ellen gave the green light. The Sunday night movie, *Dying to Be Perfect: The Ellen Hart Peña Story*, explored this hellish disease and the vicious cycles of bingeing and purging induced by both weight concerns and underlying emotional factors.

She explains, "I felt that I had been given that experience for a reason. It was as if, in a religious sense or a cosmic sense, certain things have a reason for being and you have to just leave your mind and heart open. My reason for doing the movie was very specific: I have a healthy and happy life now. Before, it was completely circumscribed by food. I also thought that as the parent of two little girls, it would break my heart to see them go through that, particularly if I thought I had been in a position to have raised awareness even a little bit."

As a result of the movie, Ellen was invited to speak at universities. It was not easy for her to get away with two young children, pregnant with a third, and Federico going through the Senate confirmation process for a new cabinet post at the Energy Department. In a scene familiar to any mother who runs the household, Ellen recounts what it was like when she left on an overnight trip. "It was an intense time. I was up until one in the morning, pregnant, writing down specific instructions for a brand new baby-sitter. Drive here. Pack the leotard. You need to pack the snack for this. Here's a birthday present for this party. And you need to go here, take this street, and then you turn left, and then you cut across that parking lot to avoid that light. I was up for two hours writing down the detailed instructions because she and I were going to be responsible for the order of things."

Despite the difficult preparations, Ellen honored her speaking commitments. "I think it's valuable to share one's experience if it might either inspire or help others in some way." Ellen sees the possibility of a new career for herself when her children are older. It might be only a dream now, but she hopes to establish an advocacy position for increasing girls' self-esteem and body image through athletics. Ellen moved to Washington for her husband, but the move may have started her on a fulfilling career path of her own.

For Norris Mailer, the media proved much harder to control than the home front that she so ably commands. She knew when she met Norman Mailer twenty-five years ago that he was "entangled" with several women, including a wife and a mistress. She knew there were five previous wives, including one he had stabbed in a domestic brawl. She knew there were seven children, including one her age. She knew Mailer was the quintessential literary bad boy, always pushing the envelope both in his writing and his public exploits. She had no idea that living with and then marrying a celebrity would mean that fame would intrude like a third person in the marriage. She had no idea that her marriage would be publicly analyzed, that she would receive threatening letters, or that her garbage would be picked through for a magazine story. This one-time, self-described "Miss Goody Two-Shoes" had never dreamed that her own name would be smeared in a national newspaper, forcing her to defend herself publicly.

Norris got her first taste of negative press when *Spy* magazine sent a reporter to comb through her garbage. "I had thrown out a bunch of old bottles of lotion, and they made this comment about how wasteful I was. They added, 'She obviously never cooks' because there were pizza boxes in the trash. Then they printed our address, which really upset me. That was unforgivable. Then I had a one-woman show that *Spy* reviewed, writing, 'Norris Mailer, who-is-a-painter-by-virtue-of-being-married-to-a-famous man.' It was just really mean."

Suddenly, in 1991 she learned that Norman was having an affair. This was not the Norman she thought she knew; she was betrayed, especially after she had defended him many times. She was not a country girl vowing to stand by her cheatin' man. "I really did leave, [then] . . . I came back to New York and said, 'I'm not going to deal with this.' We went out to dinner so I could tell Norman the news that I was moving out, but somehow before the end of dinner he convinced me not to."

What did he say that changed her mind? "It's bizarre. My script was 'Screw you. I'm leaving. I'm going to make another life for myself.' Then I thought: 'I like this life. I like my kids.' I liked him; I was in love with him. I didn't really want to leave him. It was the situation I couldn't deal with." She adds with a shrug, "I probably wanted to stay just to see what he was up to. With Norman every day is something new."

While she did forgive him, it took two years before he regained her trust. Life had just recaptured some of the familiar rhythm when news of the private affair made gossipy headlines, and Norris, not only Norman, was suddenly the target. Actress Carole Mallory peddled a steamy memoir, boasting about her celebrity lovers, including Norman Mailer. Norman publicly admitted his infidelity, telling a

Florida newspaper, "I'm guilty of a few extramarital episodes over the years and Carole was one of them. Now, at age seventy-two, these are matters to regret since I adore my wife and was much in love with her even when I was being unfaithful."[3]

Norris could not keep silent when the *New York Daily News* ran a column about the Mallory work-in-progress, and so Norris composed a letter. The newspaper ran excerpts: "If Carole Mallory suggests that I knew and approved of her, that is a complete and outrageous fantasy. As soon as I discovered these infidelities, I believe my words to my husband were something on the order of, 'You may sleep with as many women as you wish, but you will not live with me and do it.' Since we are still together, his decision is evident."[4]

Norris shook her head, silver earrings dangling. "Of course," she told us, "the columnist chopped the letter up and didn't put in what I really had intended to say." The *Daily News* incident taught her it's pointless to try to stop a media steamroller. "There's no way to fight it. No matter what you do they're going to screw you, so the best thing is to try and be above it. If they know you're going crazy then they win. If you're going to go crazy, then do it by yourself and don't let them know." She says with determination, "I try not to go crazy."

Tested twice recently, she stood her ground. Norman's book, *The Gospel According to the Son*, written in the first person of Jesus, provoked jeers from some reviewers. Norris took a "don't-get-mad-get-even" attitude. "They were some of the ugliest reviews I ever saw. I usually read reviews at least enough to know what they're going to say. I read the nasty ones so I know who not to be nice to next time we meet."

In early 1997, Adele, the wife Norman stabbed, wrote a tell-all book of their years together with tales of sex, drugs, and violence. The children, especially Adele's daughters, Betsy and Danielle, circled around Norris, worried that she would be hurt by the stories. Instead Norris counseled the children: "You can't bad-mouth someone's mother to them no matter what they do. You know that's the whole Baptist philosophy: You don't gossip and you don't say mean things about people. The girls and I have talked about Adele's book, and they know I'm not happy about it. But I said, 'That was your mom and dad's relationship, and that has nothing to do with me, and nothing to do with you and me.'"

She pauses and then repeats a mantra that she has adopted in recent years: "Tomorrow there will be another headline. You try to rise above it. You can only be as upset as you allow yourself to be. People can't do anything to you unless you let them."

Her perspective on life colors her outlook. Norris explains, "Every long relationship is filled with small and large joys and betrayals and crises along with the day-to-day constancy of routine, and ours is no exception." At the core of her ability to navigate life's curves is a strong sense of self-esteem. "It might sound corny, but I credit my parents with a lot. I was an only child. We had no money; we didn't have an indoor toilet until I was seven. My family was real stable with a strong mom and dad. We went to church every week, and I really felt loved. That firm foundation doesn't go away just because you move to another town, just because that town's New York."

While Norris had to face a barrage of bad press, Cookie Johnson's experience was 180 degrees different. Her long-term-boyfriend-finally-turned-husband was the high-profile darling of the NBA and the press. When Magic Johnson learned in 1991 that he was HIV positive, he and Cookie had to decide whether or not they should make a public announcement. They chose—together—to face the media so they could send a message about the importance of safe sex and monogamy. Eight weeks pregnant with their first child, Cookie listened as doctors discussed Magic's condition. Although her first HIV test was negative, months would pass before a second, conclusive test was taken. Magic and Cookie had finally married only two months earlier after a fourteen-year, on-and-off relationship that began when they were college sweethearts in Michigan.

We first met Cookie looking svelte in a white-and-violet sweater set on the terrace of a Los Angeles restaurant. Her hair was sleeked back in a simple yet stylish ponytail, looking like a typical Southern California carpooling wife and mom. Cookie's outward appearance is still calm and collected as she reflects back to that period when "everything kind of stopped." She had lived an ordinary life as a buyer for a department store before moving to California a year prior to getting married. She had refused to be interviewed, trying to keep out of the spotlight. That press conference was the first time she had stepped out of the shadows, and it happened in the most emotionally difficult period of her life.

Cookie's life changed forever that day. "Earvin," as she prefers to call him, rebounded quickly from the shock, but it took Cookie longer to find the strength to deal with the reality. Her emotional recovery was helped by the good news: neither she nor her baby was HIV positive. That too was not private: the announcement was made in December 1991 by NYU's AIDS Research Center. Then she had to endure magazine interviews in which her sex life was the topic of discussion. Reporter after reporter asked whether the couple hugged, kissed, made love? If so, how?

Some women might file for divorce; others might seek therapy. Not Cookie: she preferred the old-fashioned way. Cookie confesses that it was her deep religious roots—she attends a Pentecostal church—that helped her endure. "For myself, in everything I deal with, I turn to my Bible. That's the first thing I did. That's where I got my strength. I started reading and praying, and the Lord gave me strength and told me to be strong. It worked and I had peace about it. God has always been in my life and a part of my life." And, in a life-affirming move, she and Magic adopted a little girl, Lisa, two and a half years after her healthy son, EJ, was born.

Cookie tries relentlessly to make their lives as normal as possible, but it doesn't always happen. She knew from the get-go that life with Magic would never be routine.

Although Magic has retired from basketball, he's still on the road overseeing his company, which owns movie theaters. "While he's away—even when he's in town—he's still busy, working all day long. I like to be a hands-on mother. I do have nannies, but I still like to be in control. I'm still the main caretaker. I still pick them up at school all the time and take them to school. I run my family and the household."

Nine years after that news conference, Cookie says that Magic's medical problems actually brought them closer together instead of driving them apart. It is no secret that women and men process things very differently; the Johnsons are no exception. Each had to deal with this horrifying news in his and her own way, drawing strength from one another. "He's not that kind of person who just lies back and wallows in misery. I can wallow a little bit. But I guess being with him and watching him, I just followed his example. It was like a negative thing for a half second, and he turned it into a positive thing just as fast. That is the way we've lived our lives ever since."

❧ Coping with . . . Infertility ❧

Loyita Woods likes to say she married "the first time for love, the second time for life." What's intriguing is that she married the same man twice! Talk about learning from the lessons of the past. Loyita says she certainly did. The story begins, appropriately enough, in Hollywood when fourteen-year-old Loyita developed a crush on her ballroom dance partner, Bob, an "older" man of seventeen. A few years later, in 1969, Loyita discovered they were both students at Long Beach State College and part-time employees at Disneyland. She tracked Bob down only to find he was about to leave for Fort Bragg, North Carolina, to train as a Green Beret. Undeterred, she started writing him letters, telling of her travels as a dancer with a Disney touring show. The pen-pal relationship continued and when he returned from Vietnam, the romance blossomed and they were soon married.

Bob got his old job back as a guide on the Disneyland Jungle Cruise and took acting classes on the GI bill, and Loyita was under an acting contract to Columbia Pictures Television on a series, *The Life and Times of Eddie Roberts*. Then Bob had one lucky break after another and landed a role on the TV soap *One Life to Live* in New York. Loyita encouraged him to go, even though she couldn't leave L.A.

because of her contract. What seemed doable—a weekend marriage—wasn't, and after more than eight years of marriage the couple divorced.

Four years passed and neither had a lasting romantic relationship. Bob became a hit on the soap while Loyita's acting career was "in the trash can," as she puts it, for two years following the divorce. Then she began to work rather consistently in guest star roles on several television series. She was performing in an L.A. theater production when, one night, Bob appeared at her dressing-room door and asked her out for coffee. The date turned into a marriage proposal of sorts. Loyita recalls the conversation: "He said, 'Nothing is working out for me. I always compare everyone to you, and I have a feeling you're doing the same. Maybe we just needed time.'

"We were married very young, especially by today's terms. I was twenty-two and he was twenty-five when we first married. I think that we both needed some life experience under our belts separate and apart from each other. He said, 'I think I'm looking for you and I think you're looking for me, why don't you come back to New York for six months. We'll live together, we'll go to counseling, we'll see if we can work this out, and we'll make a decision.' What we both really wanted in the end was a family. We wanted children desperately. I always thought he would make the perfect father. So I said, 'You're on!'"

But for Loyita the decision to move back to New York was suddenly complicated when she was offered a recurring role on *Night Court*, a hit sitcom at the time. She turned down the dream job to remarry and move to New York. Her priorities had shifted. Stardom was no longer important; married life was. She explains, "I had had a sense of celebrity with the consistency of the work and some of the other shows that I had been with, and it was never important to me. It just wasn't. I've never felt the need to be a star. It was never my objective. I enjoyed the work. I enjoyed the process. It's just wonderful—but it's not something I want to sacrifice my weekends with my husband or family for."

Loyita and Bob married the second time around in 1985. Starting a family became their common goal, but it was a heartbreaking journey. After a miscarriage because of an ectopic pregnancy, Loyita entered an in-vitro program, but lost the baby in her fourth month. "We ended up having another split. I think it was because he was so devastated by the fact that he might never be a father, and I don't blame him for that at all," says Loyita. "I was so depressed I just said, 'Go, get your loft in Soho and go.' We were separated maybe for two months and he came back and said, 'No, this is not what I want at all.'"

About eighteen months later, they entered an in-vitro program again and became pregnant, this time with twin boys. The twins were born prematurely, six-and-a-half months into the pregnancy. "Our one son had tremendous problems and ultimately lost his battle and died a month later," Loyita says. "At first you say, 'This is our child, we will do anything on the planet that we have to do.' But then knowing the suffering this child would have to endure, we knew he would be in a much better place and things took their natural course. Bobby and I clung to each other. To have gone through that, I think, is one of the reasons why we had such a strong relationship during that period of time."

While their other son, Tanner, had problems as well, his were not irreparable. At just under five pounds, he went home from the hospital two months later. When we met Loyita she told us he is now a "normal, happy child," enjoying the summer at baseball camp. "I think we appreciate that we were able to have a child—I can't have any more. For the first five years, I totally gave him every ounce of attention. He's our life. We're a pretty special family, and hopefully, we are instilling all of the values and work ethics that we grew up with."

Anna, Ellen, Norris, Cookie, and Loyita: at different times and to varying degrees, each of these women found the extraordinary energy, inner strength, and can-do attitude to help them cope with situations ranging from slightly disturbing to seismic. Where do these women—and all women who survive such troubles—find the inner strength? The answers are as varied as the women, with Cookie and Norris bracketing the range. Cookie looked outward to the Bible for spiritual guidance, finding solace in the scriptures. Norris was fortunate enough to have a firm foundation laid during her childhood that gave her the self-confidence to face life's challenges head-on. As she sits on her deck overlooking the Provincetown bay, she reflects, "When one is asked how one deals with unpleasant situations, there is no concrete answer. Each situation has its own solution, but the old adage 'This too shall pass' is comforting, as are all old adages such as 'Nobody ever said it had to be fair' and 'Time heals all wounds.'"

To cope with the difficulties that mire any marriage, the new traditional wife draws from an emotional well for strength and courage. That well is filled with the love, friendship, trust, and commitment that come from marriage to a partner, best friend, lover, soul mate, and father of your children.

6

Unexpected Rewards

Women like giving gifts. We really do. We shop 'til we drop for the perfect present while men often grab the first thing in sight. We get an adrenaline rush from the minute we buy the present until the wrapping is ripped off. We delight in the act of giving. Many of us live the adage "It's better to give than to receive." It's the same with relationships, especially with our husbands and children.

When a woman makes a decision to marry, there certainly is an element of giving up, from her last name to old single habits. The same holds true for men. For a marriage to work, both men and women must make changes—and change continually through the years. What works for a newly married couple doesn't work for a couple with young children, and that doesn't work for a couple whose children are grown. It's constant change, and sometimes it seems—to us—that wives change and give more than husbands.

Often young, successful women and men resist this idea of change, of giving to the other person. The notion of giving up individual needs for the sake of the couple seems to have fallen out of favor. "You want me to change *my* lifestyle?" Sacrificing for the sake of the couple went the way of the Edsel when "it's all about me" became the mantra and self-absorbed Ally McBeal became the poster girl.

Nonetheless there are still many women who willingly give to their husbands of their own volition. When we give a gift to our husbands, whether it is tangible like a sweater or intangible like emotional support, we must ask ourselves, "Is this something he really wants?" In his book, *Living the 7 Habits: Stories of Courage and Inspiration*, Dr. Stephen Covey tells of a woman who, in an effort to do something special for her husband, decided to launder the family wash perfectly and keep the kids squeaky clean. Despite the efforts of Dr. Covey's "Superwasherwoman,"[1] her husband didn't even notice! She finally realized that while she was pleased, her husband, on the other hand, didn't care about smooth sheets or clean jeans.

The family CEOs emphasized that their husbands, too, approached their marriages with a sense of giving, willing to put in long hours at the office, to help with the children and chores, and to subsume some of their needs for the greater good of the shared life. Their marriages are egalitarian, not necessarily in division of labor but in the sense of partnership. No one is sitting with a clipboard, checking off "wife cooked dinner, so husband must clean up."

Gift giving is a reflection of a certain attitude toward marriage. The women we talked with enjoyed giving; indeed, they sought out new ways to give. "I do everything" is the common chant. That sentence can be a boast, a complaint or a proud statement. For these women, it is the last. They give the gift of themselves to their husbands and children. Many do it without expecting anything back. They want to take care of their families; they get pleasure in that work.

It's also reflected happiness, allowing a husband time to focus on his work. Many women told us, "Yes, I run the errands and pay the bills, things he might do on a Saturday if I insisted. But now on Saturdays he takes the kids to the park to play, and I enjoy seeing him having fun with our children. And we're not too exhausted on Saturday night to go out as a couple." Many of the women were surprised at how much satisfaction they received from doing for others. They gave a gift because they derived pleasure—yes, pleasure—from the very act of giving. They were delighted, some even stunned, at the unexpected dividends they received in return.

◌ Giving and Getting ◌

This idea of giving and getting raised some very interesting issues for both of us. When we were honest with each other, we admitted that there are times when we give a gift that we do expect something in return. If we give a birthday gift to a friend, when our birthday rolls around it would be disappointing not to get something, no matter how small. Doing a favor for a friend is also a kind of gift giving: watching a friend's toddler when her baby-sitter bails at the last minute, picking up a prescription for a neighbor with a sick child, lending the perfect evening bag. The examples are endless. While most times we are happy to help, there is a piece of us that expects that we can call on that person when we get caught in a bind.

Still, there are endless times when we "do" for our husband and children, parents and friends and expect zero in return. If we get something back it's a complete surprise. We met two women, Maggie Hoffman and Pat Findlen, who generously turned their lives upside down for the sake of their husbands' careers, not looking for any reward. Although completely different, each unforeseen payoff was priceless.

When Pat Findlen's husband, Dr. Paul LeBlanc, was offered the presidency of Marlboro College in southern Vermont, she urged him to accept the offer, even though it would make her life more difficult. At the time, Pat and Paul were living in Springfield, Massachusetts, where she was a partner in a three-person law firm and he was a publishing executive. Paul was not looking for a new job; it found him. In January 1996, Marlboro College, a small, innovative, liberal arts school, sought Dr. LeBlanc as a candidate for its presidency. As the yearlong process progressed, it became clear that if Paul was offered the prestigious position, Pat's life would change dramatically too. "Careful what you start," Pat, forty-four, told us laughing. "Next thing you know you are moving to Vermont."

When the search committee's large pool dwindled down to the final candidates, Pat was brought in and given the once-over at faculty-student luncheons. "When it was down to three candidates they wanted to lay eyes on you," she says. Realizing that "the wife of" was a job that came with expectations and responsibilities, Pat felt compelled to go on record: Yes, she would move onto the college campus. No, she would not prepare elaborate, home-cooked dinner parties. "I don't cook," she candidly told the search committee. "I *really* don't cook." But she does host dinners—catered cuisine, of course—in their home, an old farmhouse. "I signed on for that," she says.

Paul got the job, but what about Pat's practice? She realized that she could move from her home but not leave her job. So the family now lives on the Vermont campus and Pat commutes 144 miles round-trip to her Massachusetts' law firm.

Pat was willing to give the gift of the long hours behind the wheel so that Paul could become a college president. Initially Pat expected little in return for her efforts, but she soon realized the entire family benefited from this move. Because Marlboro College attracts many extraordinary people to its campus, Pat, Paul, and their two daughters meet renowned scholars who, most likely, would not have otherwise crossed their path. They have hosted fascinating visitors from around the world, including Nobel Peace Prize winner Jody Williams, scientist E. O. Wilson, and award-winning author James Carroll. "The opportunities for the kids are just endless," says Pat. "The entertaining we do in our house includes novelists, musicians, writers. I didn't count on this set of things. They are invaluable."

But Pat knows a college presidency is not forever. So what's next for Paul? With a Ph.D. in English and a specialty in technology, Paul will undoubtedly have many more exciting opportunities and offers. "Something else will happen," says Pat, adding, "but chances are it won't be in driving distance of Springfield."

Maggie Hoffman's story is an example of fact being stranger than fiction: a chance encounter on a plane, a single mom with three kids, a South African doctor with a passion for healing, and best of all, an unexpected, magnanimous gift. It all started when Maggie agreed, with great trepidation, to be matron of honor at her sister's wedding in Chicago. Separated from her husband, Maggie was a single mom living in New York with three children—one-year-old Rosie and three-year-old twins, Molly and Jacob. Maggie, thirty-four at the time, couldn't just leave the kids with a baby-sitter and a list of emergency contact numbers. Her twins had been born prematurely at twenty-seven weeks and had residual difficulties: Molly was blind, prone to seizures, and fed intravenously through a catheter; Jacob has high-functioning autism and mild cerebral palsy. Child care didn't mean hiring a local high school student; for Maggie's twins it meant full nursing care.

After military-like maneuvers, Maggie managed to arrange baby-sitters and make it to the wedding. She almost missed her return flight, resorting to changing out of her organza bridesmaid's gown in the cab. Finally aboard the plane, she slid into her airline seat comforted by strawberry Twizzlers in one hand and a trashy novel in the other. It was there that life, true to form, took a turn when Maggie least expected it. "The plane takes off and all of a sudden this incredibly attractive hairy forearm crawls across the book and a voice with this remarkable accent says, 'I'm Darryl Hoffman,'" she recalls, smiling about the memorable moment. "I still had a vestige of female-connectedness enough to stash those Twizzlers and the book under the seat and turn around and say, 'Hi. I'm Maggie.' He was so nice. But, of course, like a normal person, I spill about my kids in the first second, and how wonderful they are and show pictures. In that first hour, I'm still being that children's mother and thinking, 'Who can I set this man up with?' But by the second hour, I'm never letting him know that there was any woman between the ages of fourteen and eighty. I was over-powered by him."

Darryl turned out to be a physician doing his cardiac fel-lowship in a Bronx, New York, hospital. Forty-eight hours later when he called to ask her out (she was waiting by the phone like an adolescent), Maggie was ecstatic. Their first date, almost nine years ago, was an outing to the Bronx Zoo, not far from the hospital. One date followed another. Sometimes they would eat a home-cooked dinner while he monitored sheep in which he planted new mitral valves. Other times a date meant Maggie picked him up at an air-port—in her wheelchair van—late at night while her kids were asleep. Maggie even admits to cleaning his apartment before his mother's arrival from South Africa. "I was the geisha girlfriend. He was a wonderful person. If I could make his life easier, why not?"

We couldn't help wondering why Maggie, now forty-three, would willingly take on another role in her already oversubscribed life, even if she was madly in love. "My belief is part of love is the recognition that everyone likes to be taken care of," she explains. "Why wouldn't I want to give things to this man I was crazy about? And he was never ask-ing for it, but it gave me pleasure—and it still does—to make his life easier because of what he was doing. I thought of it, and still do, as being of paramount importance. But I also believed that because there were many people in my life who needed tremendous accommodations, I wanted him to know that I loved him. One of the ways that I could show him was by doing special things. But that was totally my choice."

After a few months, Darryl asked to meet her kids. As Maggie says, "I didn't just have kids." She had twenty-four-hour nursing for Molly, a nanny to help with the other two children, as well as physical therapists, occupational therapists, speech therapists, even feeding therapists. At that point Maggie was giving all she could in time and love to Darryl, but she wasn't letting him get close to the children. "He used to say to me, 'I'm really impressed with how you can cubbyhole everything and keep us separate, but it's making me feel uncomfortable.'"

In December 1992, Maggie and Darryl married; three months later Molly died. Then something extraordinary happened: Darryl adopted Jacob and Rosie. "Talk about getting a gift in retrospect," says Maggie, "a surprise gift; a new father for your children. That was the surprise to me. I never expected that. I expected to have to segment my life always."

᠊ᠬ Taking Turns ᠆

Sometimes giving and getting means taking turns with our husbands. Despite the high divorce rate in the United States, many young women we met anticipated long, loving marriages, so they willingly put their careers on hold, believing their turn would come later. They think of it as reciprocity. What we heard over and over was: "This is his time, but I am entitled to mine later."

Taking turns does not always mean the distant future. Although Kathy Scheller is still clearly the family CEO, her husband, Brad, willingly takes complete charge of their three boys on weekends while she studies for her nursing exams.

Other wives cited examples of taking on volunteer or part-time work assignments that swelled to unforeseen proportions. Their husbands stepped in to assume additional responsibilities, from making dinner to taking over bath time to grocery shopping to running errands. For these couples, taking turns, either sporadically or permanently, is simply an extension of the partnership approach to marriage.

Let's be clear: many of these husbands already—willingly and happily—help with the children and house. Taking turns means assuming additional responsibility. Mary's husband's longtime habit was to go to his office every Saturday morning for a few hours. He changed his Saturday routine so Mary could have an extended quiet time to work on this book. He went in earlier on weekdays, stayed home Saturdays, and on Sundays he took their young daughter and a friend to the beach. "For him there was no question that he would step in so that I could have the time to write a book. That's what partners in marriage do for each other."

For Loretta, patience was the key to getting her turn. Loretta had been passionate about teaching, her post-college career, but walked away from the classroom when she had her first child. "When I gave birth to my daughter there was no way that I could be available to my students the way I used to be. My husband was an associate in a large law firm, working wacky hours. I was a young mother who had very little experience with babies. I saw no choice but to leave teaching and make my own family a priority.

"I was married at twenty-one and a mom by twenty-three, young by today's standard. An inner strength and trust in my husband allowed me to believe and say to myself, 'My turn will come.' It took twenty-five years to get my chance to launch a new career, one that excited me the way the classroom did. But don't think for one minute that it was all diapers and bottles during the in-between years. For more than a dozen years, I worked part-time in a travel agency as well as serving on numerous museum boards, coupling my interest in education and the arts.

"By that time my children were grown. My husband took a leave from corporate America for a spell, so it was my turn. Like a VCR, I went in fast-forward, working to reach my dream of becoming a published journalist. After an internship at *Travel & Leisure* magazine, I took a job as special correspondent at *Live,* an entertainment magazine, where I wrote almost monthly, building a fat portfolio in record time.

"Writing some fifty articles since getting my master's in journalism in 1994 has not been easy. I've had late nights at the computer, early morning planes to catch, and those dreaded 'writer's block' moments. And as an older, fledgling journalist, sometimes I work a bit slower than ace reporters, but even that doesn't bother me. I love reporting and writing and it was worth the wait."

Like Loretta, Norris Mailer started out in the classroom. Before she met Norman she had been a high school art teacher as well as an avid painter. After her marriage she continued to paint and had several one-woman shows. As the children left home, she felt compelled to earn more money. The main gallery for her paintings had closed; the cost of raising and educating nine children had battered their financial standing.

Enticed by the book and screenplay deals that some of her friends had made, Norris began to devote at least four hours a day to writing. Norris found Norman's energy and drive an inspiration as she embarked on yet another career as a screenwriter and novelist. She doesn't seem to care about her picture on celebrity pages in newspapers and magazines anymore. "He's getting more serious about his work, and I am too about mine," she told us. "It's congenial to work like that together and go through compatible cycles in your life. There's not a lot to do in P-town, so we work all day, have dinner, watch a little TV, and go to bed. I don't want to go back to the party cycle anytime soon."

While several screenplays were optioned, her dream was to write a novel. Norris set a goal: a published novel before age fifty. Yes, she made her deadline with the publication of her novel, *Windchill Summer*, set in 1969 Arkansas. She wrote us, "After twenty-five years with Norman, I have found a calling as a novelist—it seems like fifty is the year to begin a whole new life."

Both Norris and Loretta took turns with their husbands, a his-time-her-time scenario. Marlene Wynne sees it differently. She sees more than thirty years of marriage to Bob as a shared giving and getting. She explains, "I feel that every time Bob has accomplished a plateau and taken a turn, it's been my turn too. I've benefited from that. I haven't felt that it's only his turn in becoming very successful. We can enjoy his huge success and that's our turn together. Right now, it's my turn and his turn. We don't have the day-to-day responsibilities of our children, even though they have adult problems just like us. We can enjoy the grandchildren. That's our turn together."

Some social commentators don't want to acknowledge relationships like the Schellers, Quigleys, Mailers, Kaufmans, and Wynnes. They want us to believe that women are always giving and men are always getting. We have not found this to be true. It was certainly not the case in Shelley Draheim's marriage. It was Shelley's husband, Jim, who jumped through hoops so she could work part-time after their daughter was born in 1991. "When we had our first child I was dumbstruck by how much I wanted to spend time with her," Shelley wrote in an e-mail. "We have always supported each others' goals and wishes, trying not to hold one another back." Living in a Washington, DC, suburb, Shelley worked as a full-time government relations specialist and research assistant during her older daughter's first year. "I dropped her off at 6:00 A.M. and picked her up at 6:00 P.M.," says Shelley, who squeezed out an hour in the evenings to bond with her baby. "I missed her first year. I kept asking myself, 'Why did I have this child if I am never going to see her?'"

She hit upon the solution—moving back to her hometown of Omaha, Nebraska, where her family still lived. Her husband got a transfer with an architectural firm, and Shelley, after giving birth to a second daughter, job shared a research position at the Greater Omaha Chamber of Commerce. "We made big sacrifices to move so that we could afford for me to work part-time. But my life was wonderful. I job shared with a partner. We even shared day care. My girls were with their grandparents one day a week. It was perfect."

Jim gave Shelley a priceless gift and she savored those six years, more time to be with each other, their children and extended family. Then the tables turned. In 1996, Jim got a job offer that meant returning to the Washington area. "His company said, 'Go back East and manage an office,'" she says, explaining that the move would put him on a fast track in his architectural firm. "If it was my career and I knew that there was a similar opportunity for me, I would take it. I was nervous, yet I knew it was important for my husband not to go through life and look back and regret that he didn't take the opportunity. We always supported one another that way. I realized if the tables turned he would do it for me." Shelley and Jim moved to Burke, Virginia, but this time Shelley decided that she would not look for another job. She told Jim, "I hate to put it all in your lap, but I don't want to have to find a job because it would be so stressful." Shelley said that she did not want to deal with finding a place to live, schools, and sending out resumes all at the same time. Also part-time research assistant jobs are not exactly easy to come by.

It took two years after moving back in 1996 before Shelley was finally comfortable with her decision to stay home. "I read Gloria Steinem," she says. "I was totally career oriented when I was in high school and college. I was an independent woman making my own money. The liberating side of feminism is the ability to make choices: the choice to be a lawyer or doctor and the choice stay home, raise good kids, and help them grow into adults who are respected." Every year on her birthday for the last decade, Shelley has made a point of reflecting on the past year of her life. "I'm turning thirty-seven. What I have done with my life?" she asked this year. "I had to ask myself, 'Did I change the world?' I'm not a surgeon saving lives. Instead I'm building two lives here."

The joys of full-time mothering have been one reward, but the truly unexpected gift is a stronger, more loving marriage. "It's been a great growing experience," Shelley says. "I am enjoying staying home and getting over the hump that it's okay to do this. It has strengthened our relationship. I'm more dependent on him, which is good. Perhaps because my parents divorced, I kept this little wall between us; I never took his advice. Now I do."

Carol Rolnick has been on both ends of giving and getting. She gave up a career that encompassed many jobs, from hospital administrator to dolphin trainer, to be the full-time family CEO. Her presence at home was not only for her children but also to lighten the stress on her husband, an emergency-room physician. As her children got older she had offers of part-time work. Her husband encouraged her to follow her put-aside passion for writing instead. She has written one travel guide and hopes to get two novels published. But Carol is a realist. If the writing does not prove to be financially feasible she will find other work.

Carol repeated a feeling we heard expressed from other women. Many husbands had originally assumed their lifestyle was based on a dual-income marriage. When the couple decided that the wife would stay home, there were consequences for both husband and wife. The wife back-burnered her career; the husband assumed full responsibility for supporting the family. Staying home also certainly puts a dent in long-term savings. As the children age and the $100,000 college degrees loom, many new traditional wives see returning to work as not only a way to resume a career but also a chance to lighten the financial burden on their husbands. As Carol's teenage children approach the college years, she says, "I feel some pressure to be more financially productive because my husband has carried the ball all these years. I would like to be earning something and have a sense of pulling my own weight, not leaving it all to him."

⌒ The Joy of Giving Back ⌒

By putting her career on hold and taking time out to raise her family, Rosanne Breen found an added meaning and purpose in her own life. She wants her children to understand the responsibility we have as citizens to give something back to society, to feel a sense of community. What better way to teach than by example? Rosanne, a little overqualified with a graduate business degree, volunteers as a teacher's aide in her daughter's elementary school, working one-on-one with students who need help with math. However, her work as a Brownie leader, teaching the positive precepts of scouting, hits the message home to her daughters. "I enjoy doing creative projects with them and working to help them understand the benefits of community service," she explains. "Most important, I hope they see how girls can do anything."

Cookie Johnson has also found added meaning and purpose through her volunteer work at The Magic Johnson Foundation, which she started with her husband. "It's like a passion to help people," Cookie says, speaking from her heart. Her commitment is unquestionable. "I haven't really worked a 'job,' but I do a lot of work with the foundation now, speaking engagements and things like that. I'm very involved," says Cookie.

Her time commitment has steadily increased as her children have gotten older. From a black-tie dinner in Lansing, Michigan, that helped her mother-in-law raise funds for local charities to the "Magic Bowl," a fund-raising event during Super Bowl weekend, Cookie's calendar is full. The Johnsons' high profile has gathered celebrity support for the foundation, including a fashion show with Elizabeth Taylor that raised $4 million for California HIV/AIDS organizations. Cookie serves as vice president of the board of directors and uses her expertise as a former retail clothing buyer for fund-raising projects. "Right now we are planning a fashion show and it's going to be at our house," explains Cookie.

The Magic Johnson Foundation has branched out and enlarged its mission beyond AIDS/HIV education programs, awarding more than $10 million in grants to remedy educational, health, and social problems affecting inner-city children. "Our mission is to help as many people as we can," Cookie says.

For Maggie Hoffman, giving to others also extends beyond her children and her husband, a cardio-thoracic surgeon. For ten years she has been the facilitator of a support group for the parents of children needing chronic care. Even more impressive, she and two other mothers started Project DOCC (Delivery of Chronic Care), which provides training for pediatric residents in the care of children with constant, special health needs. The program, taught by parents, emphasizes dealing with the children's emotional and physical needs as well as those of their families. Maggie seems to be in perpetual motion, trying to make Project DOCC a part of every pediatric-resident–training program in the country, caring for her own children, and working twenty hours a week at a local hospital—and she still makes her husband a priority in her life. "My husband is passionate about healing people," says Maggie. "He is passionate about what he does. And that's part of the spark that's always been there for us— that people passionate about something need other people like that. I've known always that what he does has to be sacrosanct, special, apart, and always able to continue. Just because I have a mission [Project DOCC] that informs every breath that I take, that doesn't change the fact that our family really was built on the premise of keeping him and what he does moving forward. That can't, that didn't, change in the deal.

"My husband always respected who I was as a person, how I took care of my kids, how I am involved in disabilities. But his respect for me and our partnership has grown since I've done what I've done with Project DOCC, there's no two ways about it. We are a better partnership, even though we are both working harder."

Nina Salkin found new meaning and purpose for her life in a religion that she was born into but didn't really embrace until she married Jeff, a rabbi. Their story, like Maggie's, begins with an accidental meeting. Jeff had time to kill before catching a train to Doylestown, Pennsylvania, where he was the rabbi of a small congregation, so he stopped, unannounced, at the midtown office of Nina, an old college chum. Nina says, "Jeff wandered into my life in a fairly accidental way, but now that I live in Jewish rhythms and Jewish spiritual time, I think there was something *beshert*, something foreordained, meant to be."

Within a year, they married and Nina straddled two worlds: the Big Apple on weekdays, temple and Torah in Doylestown on weekends, sometimes staying overnight in the city, sometimes commuting. "It was pretty grueling but I had a fantastic job," Nina says. Jeff, too, had a wonderful job, as the rabbi of a Reform congregation in a lovely but isolated town outside of Philadelphia. Nina understood how much this first solo assignment meant to her husband. "There was no cantor and Jeff played guitar. He kind of did everything. He set up the chairs, and he opened and closed the building. He was the first full-time guy and he set a pretty ambitious tone."

The commute was not the only difficult part of her new life. She tried to make small talk after the Friday night services, but she didn't exactly fit in. "It was clear to me that I had a more interesting job, not only than the women but also than most of the men. I came from having shot or cast a commercial. I wanted to talk about it with people and there really wasn't anybody to talk about it with. I think I was really unlike any other woman in the congregation and not very well integrated into that life." The other big change for Nina was her participation in the synagogue's religious life. Raised Jewish on Long Island, Nina had been to temple for few occasions other than the high holidays, weddings, and funerals. Although she wasn't required to go to services, as Jeff's wife she wanted to go and gain a deeper understanding of the rituals and their meaning.

Empathy for her newfound role came in the form of other *rebbitzen* (the Hebrew word for "rabbis' wives"), who invited Nina to join their Philadelphia-based group. "I think *rebbitzen* was a term that was rather taboo back then in the mid-'80s," Nina says. "We all saw ourselves as women of many talents, with careers and jobs. Most of us were working women and we didn't see ourselves as defined by our husbands' roles."

Nina continued the weekday-weekend routine for about eighteen months, through her first pregnancy. "I think this was the most confusing time of my life," she admits. "From the time of dating Jeff and going out to Doylestown, to then leaving my job and being full-time in Doylestown, married with a baby, was a very, very confusing time for me. It was really hard. I can remember being pregnant and sitting with my husband and saying, 'You don't understand. I'm giving up everything. Nothing is going to change for you but everything will change for me. I mean, yes, some things will change for you, but everything is going to change for me.'"

Life did change more for Nina than for Jeff. Sam was born in 1986 and Nina decided, after working briefly, to become a full-time mother. "If you have children you learn very quickly that what is demanded of you as a mother is a very consuming, big, bold, deep thing. You can choose to delegate it to somebody else. Many people do it and have fantastic children and fantastic families. Or you can do that boring day-in, day-out work, and recognize it as holy work and honor it, and take strength in it." Gradually Nina began to see the world in a different light. She wrote about the profound changes of those early Doylestown years in a column in a Jewish newspaper, *Forward*: "It certainly wasn't all bar mitzvahs and honeycake. Temple life was meetings and fierce politics, and late-night phone calls and constant ambushes in local restaurants and supermarkets. I got used to having my privacy compromised. I got used to sharing Jeff. What floored me was realizing I had married a man and a community. Our lives were tightly woven into the warp and woof of one small congregation where 'stuff' happened relentlessly. I saw a baby battle cancer, a family crumble under a father's cocaine abuse, and a young mother commit suicide. All these people needed my husband to make Jewish sense out of their chaos. And sometimes he actually could."[2]

In 1988, the family moved to Long Island where Jeff has led two large congregations. Nina, forty-six, sat with us one winter morning in her husband's library and talked about all that she did—her job, her move, caring for the children, involvement with the congregation. When Nina said, "I do" she did expect to get a loving husband for life; she didn't expect a bounty of gifts in return. "What I love about being married to Jeff is that it put me in the realm of the world of ideas," she explains. "There was always intellectual stimulation because I was married to a rabbi, and there were always guest lecturers, and there were fabulous people coming to my dinner table, and I wasn't just stuck with people talking about what video we rented last week. This was my perk. To me this was everything. This was what I couldn't have articulated but what I always wanted to do, even in my advertising years. And now I don't think it was such a sacrifice at all. I think it was a great gift to me."

As Nina watches Jeff minister to others, she finds that her own faith continues to deepen. "I've grown to really cherish the Jewish tradition," she says. "I'm not hostile to it; I don't find it burdensome. I find it beautiful and deep and meaningful. I found that there is content in Judaism that I never knew existed. And I want to know more and want to do more and I want to do it right. I want to be more authentic, more and more authentic. And I have my own live-in teacher, this man whom I love, who is my best friend, who I magically and unexpectedly fell in love with."

☙ Spirituality As a Survival Tool ❧

Through her husband's work, Nina discovered a spiritual depth she never imagined existed. We were curious about our other "amazing women," as we like to call them. We waited until we almost finished the book to broach this very personal question in an e-mail: "What role, if any, does spirituality play in your life as wife and mother?" Talk about unexpected rewards! The responses we received were truly inspirational. We were also heartened to learn that the question itself had prompted some positive soul-searching. "Yes, spirituality plays a role. Though I must be honest, until you asked the question, and I thought about it, my initial reaction was probably not," wrote Kathi Morse. "With thought, I now see that it has played a very key role."

Jennifer Ransdell expressed a similar sentiment in her e-mail: "Thanks for letting me be a part of this. You have given me a chance to write down some of what I have been thinking and feeling for years and it has helped me focus even more on my job."

The significance of spirituality varied from woman to woman. A few were blunt. "Spirituality plays absolutely no role in my life," one wrote. But for most of the women, spirituality is a sustaining and guiding force.

For some wives, spirituality helps them deal with the multiple demands on their time, talents, and energies. "Spirituality has been helpful both as a coping strategy as well as a way to help keep me centered, peaceful," Maggie Hoffman wrote. "When things are tough, I feel supported by my beliefs. When life is good, I feel more connected to nature, my 'global' community, and to God by working for those who are in a tough situation themselves."

Josephina Cervantes, who like many other mothers often finds caring for two small children more stressful than being a corporate boss, said a priest advised her to pray for patience and wisdom to fulfill her vocation as a mother. "When I don't know what to do with my screaming three-year-old, I demand the patience and wisdom from Jesus. It's worked. My faith has sustained me through the many challenges in this role," she says.

Margo Litzenberg says, "I have to admit that there are days that sometimes get so hard that without spirituality I am not sure where I would be."

Yet sometimes that same screaming child can help us grow as individuals. "I learn many spiritual lessons each day I spend with my children—lessons in patience, love, understanding, compassion, and forgiveness, to name a few," says Alison Carlson.

Spirituality can encompass both the self and the sacred. Margo describes "two levels of spirituality." She writes, "First, there is my relationship with God. The other level of spirituality is my relationship with me."

It's essential to find a "room of one's own," especially if all our responsibilities threaten to overwhelm us. It might be an occasional girls-only night out; it might be hiring a babysitter for a regular jogging or exercise time; it might be getting up early to read a newspaper or a novel. No matter the method, the purpose is to renew your spirit. "Through my own thoughts and yoga, I've spent more time and focus gaining a greater sensibility concerning my spirit and body," says Caren Osten Gerszberg, thirty-five, of Larchmont, New York. "I think I've learned—especially since having children—that inner happiness is the key to life and helps me create a more loving and secure environment for my family. It sounds like this comes from a textbook, but it's genuinely what I believe!"

The time alone is often spent on hobbies and interests that hearken back to the BC (Before Career or Before Children, as the case may be) era. "I view this 'time of one's own' as an opportunity to recharge your batteries by feeding your spirit and soul," wrote Alison Carlson, who resumed singing in a choral group when her youngest child stopped nursing. "Music has been my lifelong avocation and provides me with a great deal of joy, soulful sustenance, and personal satisfaction. As a mom at home, singing in a choral group is also a wonderful social outlet for me, and it gives me the opportunity to meet people who share this same passion with me. I cannot imagine living without this important creative outlet. This is the one thing I do in my life that is a personally rewarding, creative expression and is just for me alone— not for my husband, not for my children, not for my family." An added perk is that Alison changes out of her jeans and running shoes every once in a while to perform for an appreciative audience.

Margo Litzenberg learned the power of time alone. "If it is taking time to exercise, take a bath, or just read a good book, I can reenergize my soul, which I believe is good for *my* spirit. As a wife and a mother, this time to reflect, or be spiritual with myself, helps me to reconnect with who I am so I don't get lost. Then I feel I can go again to be with my family and help guide them through life a little better."

Shannon Purushothaman also finds spirituality in the simple pleasures. "Just lying out on the deck and watching the clouds or listening to the wind blow through the trees connects me to myself, my children, and the world. It may seem simple, but it creates such a sense of peace and connection. I look for the ordinary everyday events that go unnoticed to connect to my spirituality, which connects me to everything else."

For others, organized religion is their link to the spiritual. Becky Wilsey wrote, "As I've aged, I've also had more questions of my own and have sought direction and ideas through my church's adult education program. And especially after a trying week, it is a quiet and peaceful refuge to be in a sanctuary where people are seeking healing, community, and beauty."

Carlie Dixon found that the opportunity to explore her spiritual feelings led her to convert to Catholicism. Carlie, forty-seven, who worked as a tax lawyer for ten years, e-mailed us while vacationing on Flathead Lake in Glacier National Park, Montana. "Being a full-time mom gave me the freedom, the time, and the desire to even consider such a major move. I converted two-and-a-half years ago (nine-and-a-half years into being at home)," she wrote. "I was remarried in the Church at the same time. So my marriage is now a sacramental one and by God's grace has become much stronger, closer, and more beautiful than I ever could have imagined."

For Vicky Austin, having children caused her to examine her ethical and spiritual grounding much more closely. "Spirituality informs everything I do. When I didn't have children, I didn't have to answer questions like, 'Why did God invent mosquitoes?' and I didn't spend much time thinking about them. I have always been to some degree religious in a traditional way, and with the advent of children, I felt it was much more important to live the values I wanted to impart to the family. 'Living our values' is a sort of baseline that my husband and I return to often when making decisions."

"Living our values" was an objective that was repeated by many different women. "I see spirituality as a feeling of purpose in our lives, not just a religious question," wrote Patty Larson. "I believe that we are all here for a purpose and many of us spend much of our lives trying to find out what that purpose is. I believe each person has a different purpose. Now that I am a mother, I somehow believe that maybe my purpose is to nurture a child to become a caring person to fulfill her purpose in life, whatever that may be."

Patty continued: "I believe as a wife and mother, I play a large role in the beliefs and feelings of both my husband and daughter. I got my husband to go to church regularly. I sometimes don't realize how I affect my husband until he comments on something later. So I figure if I affect my husband that much, I must play a really big role in my daughter's life. I also believe it is important not to just believe, have faith, but to follow through with that faith. Faith is empty without works."

Kathi Morse follows her faith by abiding by the Ten Commandments. "As an individual, and a mother, I was guided by the principles of the Ten Commandments, and by virtue I taught my children to be good, caring, and thoughtful people based on those principles. As a wife that has been true as well. I have made choices based on what I think is ethical and right, looking at God's law as well as man's. I have made choices, and conducted myself, in both roles, with the idea that in some way this world will be a little bit better because I was here. I have also made choices hoping that my life and my family's life will be of value and judged to be lived well."

Dot Whalen brings a common sense approach to practicing her faith. "A priest once said that each day can begin with 'Good morning, God' or 'Good God! Morning.' I try to start each day with the former and in my first car ride of the day, I turn off the radio and pray in the silence of my car. First, I thank God for all the blessings that I have—health, happiness, a loving family—and then I pray for what I think I need. At times I pray to be a better wife, mother, daughter, sister, and at times I get completely distracted and I think about the list of things I have to do."

ᴄᴏ Finding Fulfillment As a Woman ᴄᴏ

Spirituality helps us fulfill our roles as wife and mother. How do those roles, in turn, give our lives as women meaning and purpose? We are the glue that holds our family together. We complete them. Do they complete us? Sometimes? All the time? For now? We asked two additional questions of our women's online group: "How does being a wife and mother fulfill you as a woman? Do the parts add up to more than the sum?" Again, judging by the deeply personal answers, we had tapped feelings that, while they linger in the back of our minds, are not topics we talk about every day. The choice to stay home is a decision strongly influenced by the heart as well as the mind, and the answers reflected a range of emotions.

Margo takes great satisfaction in her life now. "I believe what I do gives meaning to my life in that there is nothing more important in this world (to me) than being a good mom and a supportive wife," she wrote. "My life is identified by my child, the baby on the way, and the wife who supports her husband's career. Doing things for my family gives me a great sense of purpose in life because I am helping them to achieve what is going to bring us all to the next level. At this time, there is nothing more to fulfill me as a woman. I don't know if that sounds like craziness to anyone, but like I said that is who I am right now."

Jennifer Boutte's e-mail mirrored Margo's: "I love knowing that I have the power to make our home a wonderful place to be. I love knowing that I am in control of my future. I can choose to go back to work, or I can choose to stay at home full-time. I can get involved in whatever I choose. All of these things make me feel quite fulfilled as a woman."

Shelley Draheim recognized that the decision to stay home generates a new set of questions that we all ask ourselves from time to time. "Am I fulfilled?" she wrote. "I am definitely getting there. I still need my husband's support and acknowledgment of my contribution. I wonder what I would be doing if I had continued to work full time. I think about the bigger house, new car, and vacations we could have if I earned a real income. I think about the clean house we would have because nobody would be around to mess it up."

For Shelley, the trade-offs are worth it. Her family life is less stressed and her children appreciate her constant presence. "I can sleep at night because I did not miss my children's milestones, and I will not look back at my life and wish that I had left the office early more often. I may never be completely 'fulfilled' as I am always striving for more, but I do feel like I am doing the right thing with my life," she wrote.

Fulfilled? Karen Slora was straightforward in her answer. "On days when the kids are whiny, the house is trashed, and I am constantly called for, I do not feel fulfilled. On most days, however, I feel that I am making a home for my family and am ensuring positive memories. The meaning and purpose of my tasks is that I am trying to create a pleasant home life."

In an era where "dysfunctional" often seems to be the adjective of choice in describing a family, "ensuring positive memories" translates to much more than photos in an album.

A "pleasant home life" means raising emotionally secure children who will contribute to society.

Alison Carlson, like other mothers we interviewed, finds purpose in creating a secure home. "I view this 'mother at home' phase of my life as a very important stage of my life," she wrote. "It is a stage in which I am indispensable, unlike my role in the paid workforce. I remind myself that we only have 'temporary custody' of our children and, hence, a limited time within which to teach them those things we know to be important in life. When my nest is empty, my job will be complete, and I will be ready to move on to the next stage in my life, whatever it may be."

Many women agree with Alison that they see their role transcending their own family and affecting their community at large. "A strong family unit produces happy, creative, productive citizens," says Maggie Hoffman. "Those same family members contribute to building (and maintaining) the kinds of communities we all want to be a part of. My children see the importance of contributing to a whole, whether it's Daddy's job, Mommy's projects, planting a vegetable garden and tending it for the food bank, etcetera. We live a good life, and part of what makes it feel great is that we have built it together."

As we read through the e-mails, talked with other women—from grad students to grandmas—and spent long hours pondering the issue ourselves, we found an analogy of sorts in viewing our lives as a puzzle. No, not one of those thousand-piece brain teasers; rather a high quality, fifty-piece puzzle found in an upscale children's toy store. The pieces represent the many parts of our lives: husband, children, family, friends, work, play, education, and so on. Not every piece fits with another. Sometimes they need to be shifted around. Sometimes we have to move a piece to the side while we try to make two other pieces join together. Our lives are like that. Sometimes marriage and work mesh perfectly; other times they don't, so we shift and try to work it differently. The same with children and work or children and marriage.

Yes, life means constantly changing and readjusting to new circumstances. We all knew that. But for now—at this point in time—this lifestyle does give genuine meaning to our lives in a number of ways. And for most us, the changes have also helped us grow as individuals. "I am more patient," wrote Jayme Hicks. "I am more mindful of the wonderful things in this life. I had good time-management skills in the past, but now they are excellent. I am prettier. I take better care of myself. I am more lighthearted. I am more open-minded, and I am more compassionate."

We have repeated many times that the new traditional wife is a remarkable woman in many ways. She's also a woman who is always striving for more, like Maggie Hoffman. "I still feel like a 'work in progress,'" Maggie wrote. "I am certain that the part I play in my husband's life and career is extremely helpful to him and fulfilling to me. Encouraging his medical role and enabling him to respond to his patients' needs freely is very important work. My children are turning into people I admire and respect. I'd like to believe that they have benefited from being able to speak with me whenever they wish (and avoiding me as well). My volunteer and professional work is fulfilling far beyond my expectations. The sum is spectacular; the effort to hold it together is a challenge. I don't know—it feels like my vistas beg for harder work, and I constantly try to expand the amount of individual time I spend with each of my kids and my husband. On successful weeks I feel like a billion bucks; at other times, bright lipstick helps cover up the sheer exhaustion."

7

Brave New Women

THIS PAST FALL, just as *And What Do You Do?* was in its final stages, Mary and her husband, Frank, attended a back-to-school event and chatted with the wife of a casual acquaintance, who mentioned that she was starting a new job. After congratulating her, Frank asked, "Where did you work previously?" Seeming slightly embarrassed, she cast her eyes down and whispered, "I was a stay-at-home mom." Of course, Frank, along with Loretta's husband, Vic, so believes in the message of this book, that he launched into a pep talk on why staying home is an admirable choice.

Our book has been a journey of discovery about you, the women who proudly choose to take time out, to stay at home, some for months, others for years. Stereotypes—some fifty years out of date—still cloud the picture of who is at home in the twenty-first century. Setting out to find you, we rang doorbells only to discover that you're never home! You're out volunteering, visiting with friends, caring for relatives, joining book clubs, exploring new interests, working part-time. Yes, you're also running errands, grocery shopping, and carpooling but on a routine you control. You're the master of your universe, boss of your time and schedule. And you did find time, in the early morning or at the end of the day, to sit down and talk to us, either in person or by phone or e-mail, sharing your lives, your thoughts, and your feelings.

What quickly emerged was a portrait of the brave new women at home. You are smart, savvy, assertive. You are deeply in love with your husband and adore your children. Most of you had no intention of ever staying home. Indeed many of you worked for a few years after the first baby was born. At different times and for various reasons, you came to the conclusion that "juggling" was something best left to the circus. Some of you admitted that after five, ten, or fifteen years of work, you were left feeling that there must be more. The "more" turned out to be children, who stunned you with how quickly they changed your perception of the world.

Often with considerable conflict, you made the difficult decision to stay home. For many of you, it was like jumping off a cliff into the vast unknown. To survive, you had to completely alter the way you perceived your life as a woman, wife, mother, and worker. As you began to focus on being the center of your family, your relationship with your husband took on a new, deeper meaning. You became partners in parenthood as well as marriage.

The changes you feared turned out to be mentally and spiritually rewarding in ways you never dreamed. You shared your epiphanies—those wonderful revelations and compelling stories—with us so that other women can learn through your experiences.

What did we learn from you? A lot! Perhaps one of the most important points is to put aside preconceived notions about work, marriage, mothering. Intuitively we all know that life means change, but too often we get stuck on one path, the same old path, unwilling to deviate even when circumstances cry out for a different course. We all agreed that change is difficult, but it is very empowering when we do it successfully. You made the bold step to quit work, and you were criticized. You were honest enough to admit that while work was emotionally and financially fulfilling, perhaps there were other ways to reach those same levels of satisfaction. You were surprised to find that the choice to give yourself to your family gave you, as a woman, a deeper sense of purpose and meaning—a sense of fulfillment that some of you even called spiritual.

Unquestionably, some of you work because you need the money. We're saying: Think about it. Think it through. Sharpen your pencil. You may have more options than you're aware of. Don't be so quick to assume that you can't afford to stay at home. If you choose otherwise, we respect your decision. After all, that's the whole point about choice.

You learned to define yourself as a woman in a way that had nothing to do with your paid work. You told us that you knew the work world inside out, but it wasn't until you had time to reflect that you were able to get a second chance to figure out what you wanted to do with the rest of your lives. For some of you, the future is right at home. You have found great pleasure in making a home, volunteering, launching at-home businesses, being an integral part of your husband's career and your children's lives. Others are looking toward your forties and fifties with a sense of expectation—of gearing up, not slowing down—for a time of renewed self-discovery and meaningful work. Those of you who have already jumped back, told us again and again about the extra dose of energy and enthusiasm you bring to your jobs.

Regrets? Like the song says, you've had a few. Some of you said, "I wish I had planned for this." The planning goes hand in hand with the other regret: you wish that our culture had more respect for your decision. As the number of women taking time out increases, we hope that staying at home will be viewed as a celebrated choice. Almost fourteen million strong—more than the total population of Tokyo—you will be recognized for your contributions to your communities and families as well as the workplace. Instead of being whispered about, as this ever enlarging group of women raises its voice, it won't be long before the media gives you the recognition you deserve. Making the choice to stay home will then become part of a financial plan as well as an overall career strategy.

This journey has taken us into a new, uncharted territory, filled with wonderful discoveries. The message we send back is directed to young women who are contemplating this terrifying change of life and to all you thirty-somethings who have just made this change, and are still uncertain, feeling you have taken a slippery slope. You are not alone; there are millions of women like you who have made this same decision. What we have found is that the choice to stay home can be enlightening for both the heart and the mind. Your spiritual sense is awakened with deeper connections to both yourself and the outside world; your mind is awakened to a myriad of possibilities you never dreamed existed.

Our final message: When someone asks, "And what do you do?" be ready to respond with a strong, clear confident voice, "I do what almost fourteen million other women do. I choose to stay at home and to be a partner, wife, soul mate, and mother."

Notes

Rewriting the Rules

[1] U.S. Bureau of Labor Statistics, Department of Labor, *Current Population Survey 1998,* excerpted from unpublished marital and family tables, Table 8, collected by U.S. Census Bureau (Washington, DC, 1998).

[2] Roper Starch Worldwide, Inc., "Good News for Mother's Day: Motherhood Still Deemed #1 Measure of Success." 4 May 1999 (New York: Roper Starch Worldwide, Inc.,1999), http://www.roper.com/news.

[3] Cecelie Berry, "Home Is Where the Revolution Is" in "Mothers Who Think" column, *Salon* (online), 29 September 1999, http://www.salon.com.

[4] U.S. Bureau of the Census, "Table A3: Median Income of Married-Couple Households Including and Excluding the Earnings and Income of Wives: 1969 to 1996," prepared by U.S. Bureau of the Census, 3 February 1999, http://www.census.gov/hhes/income/mednhhld/ta3.html.

[5] Elizabeth Olson, "Americans Lead the World in Hours Worked," *The New York Times,* 7 September 1999, sec. C, p. 9.

[6] Arlie Hochschild, *The Second Shift: Working Parents and the Revolution at Home* (New York:Viking, 1989) 18.

[7] ibid., 3.

[8] Arlene Rossen Cardozo, *Sequencing* (New York: Atheneum, 1986).

[9] Dr. Xavier Amador, interview by authors, 5 March 1999, New York, New York.

Going against the Grain

[1] U.S. Bureau of the Census, "Table A-6: Age Distribution of College Students 14 Years Old and Over, by Gender: October 1947–1998," in *Current Population Survey,* U.S. Bureau of the Census (Washington, DC, 1999).

[2] The PEW Center for The People and The Press, "As American Women See It: Motherhood Today—A Tougher Job, Less Ably Done," 9 May 1997 (Washington, DC: The Pew Center for the People and the Press, 1997).

[3] U.S. Bureau of Labor Statistics, Department of Labor, *Current Population Survey*, "Table 4: Families with Own Children; Employment Status of Parents by Age of Youngest Child and Family Type (1996–97 annual averages), Families with own children; Employment status of parents by age of youngest child and family type, 1997-98 annual averages" (Washington, DC: Bureau of Labor Statistics, 25 May 1999. http:stats.bls.gov/news.release/famee.t04.htm.

[4] Tracy Thompson, "A War Inside Your Head," *The Washington Post*, 15 February 1998, sec. magazine, p. W12.

[5] Matt Williams, "Ushering Out a Sitcom and a Television Era," *The New York Times*, 6 May 1999, sec. A, p. 1.

[6] G.K. Singh, K.D. Kochanek, M.F. MacDorman, "Life expectancy at birth by race and sex: United States, 1940, 1950, 1960, and 1970–1994," *Monthly Vital Statistics Report,* vol. 45, no. 3, supp, National Center for Health Statistics (Maryland: 1996), 19.

[7] U.S. Department of Labor Women's Bureau, Labor Force Quiz A, May 1999.

[8] Rachel Lehmann-Haupt, "In Women's Groups, Back to 'Girl Talk," *The New York Times,* 11 April 1999, sec. 9, p 1.

[9] Stephanie Armour, "Executive Suites Come at a Price," *USA Today*, 17 February 1999, sec. A, p. 7.

[10] U.S. Department of Labor Women's Bureau, *Women Business Owners,* prepared by Economic Census Women-Owned Business and and Economic Census Characteristics of Business Owners, 1992.

[11] Bill Meyers, "Women Increase Standing As Business Owners," *USA Today*, 29 June 1999, sec. Money, p. 1B.

[12] U.S. Department of Labor Women's Bureau, *Economic Census Women-Owned Business,* 1992 (from "Facts on Working Women: Women Business Owners," www.dol.gov/dol/wb.public/wb_pub/wbo.htm).

[13] Ibid.

[14] National Foundation of Women Business Owners, *Home-Based Women-Owned Businesses Number and Employ Millions,* 1992 (www.nfwbo.com).

[15] Debbie Ouellet, "Freedom Means Choice," Letter of the Day, *Toronto Star,* 17 March 1999, sec. news.

Starring in a Supporting Role

[1] Contents Page introduction, "The Shadow Story of the Millennium:Women," *The New York Times Magazine,* 16 May 1999, 18.

[2] Frank Edward Allen, "What Problem? Chief Executives May Not Sympathize with Work-Family Conflicts for a Simple Reason: They Really Have Them," *The Wall Street Journal,* 21 June 1993, sec. Work and Family on the Job, R7.

[3] Linda Stroh, interview with authors, 18 July 1999, Chicago, IL.

[4] Betsy Morris and Lixandra Urresta, "It's her job too: Lorna Wendt's million dollar divorce is the shot heard 'round the water cooler," *Fortune,* 2 February 1998, p. 64.

[5] Nathan Cobb, "The Ex-Wife's Club: Lorna Wendt Plans to Wield Her $20 Million Divorce Victory over a GE Executive As a Weapon for Other CEO Spouses," *The Wall Street Journal,* 23 December 1997, sec. C, p.1.

[6] Myra Strober, interview with authors, 22 June 1999, Ithaca, NY.

[7] W. Jay Hughes, Ph.D., Georgia Southern University, "Issues Pertaining to Contemporary Career Wives," e-mail to authors, 15 June 1999.

[8] Daniel Goleman, *Emotional Intelligence: Why it can matter more than IQ* (New York: Bantam, 1995).

[9] Daniel Goleman, "Why Your Emotional Intelligence Quotient Can Matter More Than IQ, *USA Weekend,* 10 September 1995, 4.

[10] Dr. Willa Bernhard, interview by authors, spring and summer 1999. New York, New York.

[11] Marilyn Elias, "Longer workdays, less family time 2-career households now the norm," *USA Today,* 31 August 1998, section Life, p. 5D.

[12] Ibid., 5D.

[13] U.S. Bureau of Labor Statistics, Bulletin 2340 and unpublished January issues, "Women's Earnings As a Percent of Mens, 1979–1998," prepared by U.S. Department of Labor's Women's Bureau, 1999.

[14] Joe Torre with Tom Verducci, *Chasing the Dream: My Lifelong Journey to the World Series* (New York: Bantam Books, 1997) 160.

Choosing Children over Careers

[1] Iris Krasnow, *Surrendering to Motherhood: Losing Your Mind, Finding Your Soul* (New York: Hyperion, 1997).

[2] Susan Chira, *A Mother's Place: Taking the Debate about Working Mothers beyond Guilt and Blame* (New York: Harper Collins, 1998).

[3] Kathleen Gerson, interview with authors, 21 June 1999, New York, New York.

[4] U.S. Department of Labor's Women's Bureau, *Facts on Working Women* (Washington, DC: U.S. Department of Labor, April 1999).

[5] PEW Center for The People and The Press, "As American Women See It: Motherhood Today—A Tougher Job, Less Ably Done," 9 May 1997 (Washington, DC: The PEW Center for The People and The Press, 1997).

[6] UPI, "Survey Reveals Guns Among Children," 20 May 1999.

[7] National Association for the Education of Young Children/ American Psychological Association, "Op Ed," 22 April 1999 (Washington D.C: National Association for the Education of Young Children, 1999) www.naeyc.org.

Learning the Art of Coping

[1] Georgia Witkin, *The Female Stress Syndrome* (New York: 1991), 102.

[2] Ray Romano, *Ray Romano: Everything and a Kite* (New York: Bantam Doubleday Dell, 1998), 133.

[3] William Beamon, "Kiss and Tell," *The Tampa Tribune*, 18 September 1995, section Baylife, p. 2.

[4] George Rush and Joanna Molloy with Baird Jones, "Mailer Ex-Mistress Pitching H'wood on The Way They Were," *New York Daily News*, 26 July 1996, section: Gossip, p. 14.

Unexpected Rewards

[1] Stephen R. Covey, *Living the 7 Habits: Stories of Courage and Inspiration* (New York: Simon and Schuster, 1999), 123.

[2] Nina Salkin, "Married, with Congregation—The Joy and Jeopardy of Being a Rabbi's Spouse," *Forward*, 20 February 1998, 17.

About the Authors

LORETTA KAUFMAN has an M.A. in journalism from NYU. Married for almost thirty-five years and the mother of two children, she began her writing career after her children were grown. She lives in New York City with her husband.

MARY QUIGLEY is a writer who specializes in women's issues and teaches journalism at New York University where she received her M.A. She resides on Long Island with her husband and three children.

About the Press

Wildcat Canyon Press publishes books that embrace such subjects as friendship, spirituality, women's issues, and home and family, all with a focus on self-help and personal growth. Great care is taken to create books that inspire reflection and improve the quality of our lives. Our books invite sharing and are frequently given as gifts.

For a catalog of our publications, please write:

Wildcat Canyon Press
2716 Ninth Street
Berkeley, California 94710
Phone: (510) 848-3600
Fax: (510) 848-1326
info@wildcatcanyon.com
or see our website at www.wildcatcanyon.com